REIKI
The Healing Touch
First and Second Degree Manual

William Lee Rand
Including
Japanese Reiki Techniques
Hayashi Healing Guide

Notice to Prospective Students

The ability to channel Reiki energy cannot be learned by reading this manual. This ability is transferred to the student by the Reiki Master during an attunement process. Reiki attunements are given as a standard part of Reiki training. This manual will help those wanting to learn more about Reiki in order to decide if Reiki training is something they would like to take. However, its main purpose is for those who have already taken Reiki or for those preparing to take the training. See "The Attunement" in Chapter 1.

The ideas and techniques described in this manual are for the Reiki student. They are not meant to be an independent guide for self-healing. If you have a health condition and intend to use Reiki, please do so under the supervision of an enlightened medical doctor or other health care professional.

ISBN 1-886785-03-1
Library of Congress Catalog Card Number 98-84919

Published in the United States of America.

International Center for Reiki Training
21421 Hilltop St. #28, Southfield, MI 48033
Phone (800) 332-8112, (248) 948-8112 Fax (248) 948-9534
Email center@reiki.org   Website www.reiki.org

Printed on recycled paper.
Contains fibers from trees
grown in well managed forests.

Acknowledgments

This book would not be possible without the help and encouragement of many. I would like to thank the following Reiki Masters whose loving devotion has contributed to my Reiki training. I am especially grateful to the late Bethal Phaigh, my first Reiki teacher, who through her presence deepened my commitment to serve others. I would also like to thank, Diane McCumber for encouraging me to teach Reiki. Arjava Petter, Chetna Kobayashi and Shuziko Akimoto provided valuable information about the history of Reiki and the Japanese Reiki techniques. I also wish to thank the spirit of Reiki for the love and guidance I continually receive. I acknowledge all Reiki practitioners and teachers for the contributions they are making to end suffering and heal humanity.

Cover Art and Illustrations
Sheryl M. Matsko

Modeling
Connie Greba

Typesetting
Corey Bippes

The Logo

The Japanese kanji in the center of the logo means Reiki which is spitiually guided life energy. The upward pointing triangle represents humanity moving toward God. The downward pointing triangle represents God moving toward humanity. Because the two triangles are united, and balanced, they represent humanity and God working together in harmony. The inner sixteen petaled flower symbolizes the throat chakra or communication. The outer twelve petaled flower symbolizes the heart chakra or love. The complete logo represents Reiki uniting God and humanity in harmony through the communication of love.

The Logo is the Registered Service Mark of
The International Center for Reiki Training

William Lee Rand
Usui Reiki Master Lineage

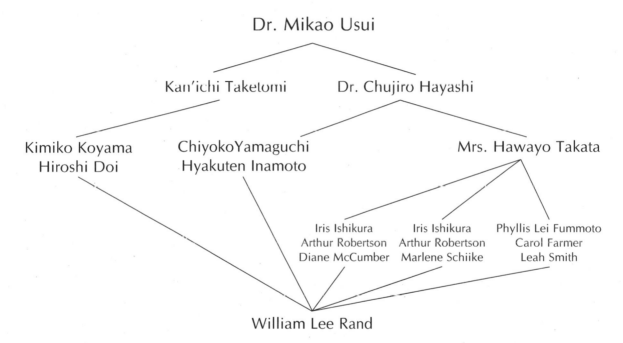

Dr. Mikao Usui

Kan'ichi Taketomi   Dr. Chujiro Hayashi

Kimiko Koyama   ChiyokoYamaguchi   Mrs. Hawayo Takata
Hiroshi Doi   Hyakuten Inamoto

Iris Ishikura   Iris Ishikura   Phyllis Lei Fummoto
Arthur Robertson Arthur Robertson   Carol Farmer
Diane McCumber   Marlene Schiike   Leah Smith

William Lee Rand

William received Reiki I in 1981 and Reiki II in 1982 from Bethel Phaigh who received her master training from Mrs. Takata. In 1989 he received the master training from Diane McCumber and Marlene Schiike and in 1991 from Leah Smith. In 2002, he received the master training in Gendai Reiki from Hiroshi Doi and also in 2002 the Komyo Reiki training from Hyakuten Inamoto. In 2001 he took Reiki I&II from Mrs. Yamaguchi and her son Tadao in Kyoto, Japan. William has taught Reiki full time since 1989 in the U.S. and in countries all over the world. He is also author of *Reiki for a New Millennium* and also co-authored *The Spirit of Reiki* with Arjava Petter and Walter Lubeck. In 1994-95, he developed Karuna Reiki®. He is also founder and president of the International Center for Reiki Training, the Reiki Membership Association and the Center for Reiki Research and publisher of the *Reiki News Magazine*. The Usui/Tibetan style of Reiki which he teaches is a combination of Japanese and Western Reiki methods.

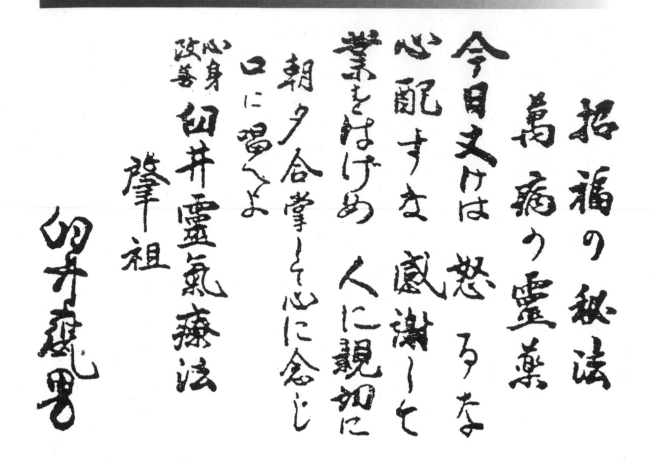

The Original Reiki Ideals

The secret art of inviting happiness
The miraculous medicine of all diseases
Just for today do not be angry
Do not worry and be filled with gratitude
Devote yourself to your work and be kind to people
Every morning and evening join your hands in prayer
pray these words to your heart
and chant these words with your mouth
Usui Reiki Treatment for the improvement of body and mind

The founder. . . Usui Mikao

See page 62 for a guide to pronouncing the Reiki Ideals in Japanese

Contents

Part I - An Overview of Reiki

Chapter 1 - Reiki Defined
Rei - Spiritual Wisdom 3
Ki - Life Energy 3
Spiritually Guided Life Energy 4
Do All Healers Use Reiki? 4
The Attunement 5
A Cleansing Process 6
Giving Reiki 6
Reiki Can Never Cause Harm 6
Reiki Never Depletes Your Energy 7
Anyone Can Learn Reiki 7
Self-Treatment 7
How Does Reiki Heal? 7
The Aura 9
The Chakras 9
The Meridians 9
What Can Be Treated? 10
Reiki Works with Medical Care 10
Is Reiki a Religion? 11
Kirlian Photography 11
Reiki Photograph 11

Chapter 2
History of Reiki 13
A More Accurate History of Reiki 15
The Inscription on the Usui Memorial 15
Dr. Mikao Usui 18
Chujiro Hayashi 21
Hawayo Takata 22
Reiki Since Mrs. Takata 25
Pictures from Mt. Kurama 27

Chapter 3
The International Center for Reiki Training 33
Scanning 33
Aura Clearing 33
Healing Attunement 33
Three-Step Session 34
Becoming a Reiki Master/Teacher 34
Holy Fire Karuna Reiki® 34
Holy Fire Reiki 34
Reiki Membership Association 34

The Center Licensed Teachers Program 35
All Reiki Groups Have Value 35
The Center Philosophy 36
The Center Purpose 36

Part II - Elements of a Reiki Session

Chapter 4
    Using Reiki 41

Chapter 5
    The Reiki Symbols 45
    Activating Reiki Symbols 47
    The Power Symbol 47
    The Mental/Emotional Symbol 47
    Healing Unwanted Habits: Weight Loss, Cigarettes, Alcohol, Drugs, etc. 48
    The Distant Healing Symbol 48
    Using the Distant Healing Symbol 50
    Group Distant Healing 51
    Empowering Goals 51

Chapter 6
    Japanese Reiki Techniques 53
    The Three Pillars of Reiki 54
    Gassho meditation.. 54
    Reiji-ho... 54
    Chiryo 55
    Byosen Scanning... 55
    Self-Scanning 58
    Koki-ho... 58
    Kenyoku.. 59
    Gyoshi-ho 60
    Jacki-Kiri Joka-ho... 60
    Enkaku chiryo 60
    Teddy Bear Technique 61
    Japanese Reiki Techniques DVD 61
    Pronouncing The Reiki Ideals In Japanese 62
    Hayashi Healing Guide 63

Chapter 7
    Hand Positions for Self-Treatment 73

Chapter 8
    Alternate Treatment for Self or Others 79

Chapter 9

Hand Positions for Treating Others 81
Beaming... 88

Chapter 10

Giving a Complete Reiki Session... 89
Developing Your Own Style 91
Techniques to Enhance the Session 91
Reiki Tables, Chairs and Tools 92

Part III - Your Own Reiki Practice

Chapter 11

Create a Thriving Reiki Practice, Part I 97
Goal Manifesting Exercise 98
Business Consciousness 99
Money Issues..100
Money Thought Experiment 100
Competition 100
Create a Thriving Reiki Practice, Part II 105
Reiki Room 106
Liability Insurance 106
Records...107
Business Expenses are Tax Deductible.......................................107
Marketing Tools 107
Email List...107
Web Site 108
Business Cards...109
Short Explanation of Reiki 109
Impromptu Reiki Sessions..110
Upward Price Technique 110
Target Fee..110
Clients Are Your Best Promoters 111
Bonus Program 111
Professional Referrals 111
Flyers 111
Magazine Advertising..111
Free Reiki Evening...111
Fundraisers 112
Holistic Fairs 112

Chapter 12

Becoming a Reiki Master 113
Reiki - A Joyful Path...113
What Is a Reiki Master? 113
Master Training Is a Serious Step..114

How to Find the Right Teacher 114
Treat Students with Great Respect 115
Set a Good Example...115
Your Life Purpose 115
The Way of Reiki 115

Appendices

Appendix A - Discovering the Roots of Reiki

Discovering the Roots of Reiki..125
Japanese Sources for Reiki History..125
Our Trip to Japan 125
Mt. Kurama - Where Reiki was Rediscovered 126
Roots of the Reiki Symbols 126
The Usui Memorial - Answers Carved in Stone 127
In Japan Fees for Treatment Are Optional...128
The Lineage of Usui Sensei 129
Helping Others Is What Reiki is All About 129

Appendix B - Reiki in Hospitals

Reiki in Hospitals 133
America's Interest in Complementary Health Care 133
Scientific Validation 134
Why Hospitals Like Reiki 134
Reiki at Portsmouth Regional Hospital...135
The California Pacific Medical Center's Reiki Program............................135
More MD's and Nurses Practicing Reiki 136

Appendix C - Reiki Training through The International Center for Reiki Training

Reiki I and II 141
Advanced Reiki Training...141
Reiki Master Training 142
Holy Fire Karuna Reiki® Training 143
Preparing for a Reiki Attunement 144
Class Schedule...144
ICRT Reiki Membership Association 145
Benefits of the RMA 145
Reiki Web Site 145
Anatomy for Reiki 146
Client Information Form..148
Reiki Session Documentation Form 149
The Beaming Reiki Masters...150
Takata's Masters...150
Reading List 151

Appendix D
  How Hawayo Takata Practiced and Taught Reiki......................157

Appendix E - Reiki Products
  Reiki News Magazine..169
  The Reiki Touch Kit 170
  Reiki Master Manual 172
  Reiki in Hospitals PowerPoint Presentation........................172
  Guided Meditation CD Kit...173
  Center for Reiki Research Booklet 173
  Healing Touch Manual - Spanish Version 173
  Reiki Membership Association.....................................174

  Reiki Membership Association Code of Ethics......................176
  Reiki Membership Association Standards of Practice 177
  Reiki II Symbol Test 178
  Class Review Form 179

Part I

An Overview of Reiki

The Japanese kanji for Reiki
Tensyo style

Chapter 1
Reiki Defined

Reiki (pronounced ray-key) is a Japanese technique for stress reduction and relaxation that also promotes healing. It was discovered by Mikao Usui in March 1922. Reiki is administered by "laying on hands" and techniques such as this have been practiced for thousands of years. Reiki is a very simple yet powerful technique that can be easily learned by anyone.

The word Reiki comes from Japanese kanji. Kanji are ideograms used in the written language of Japan. They originally came from China and are based on simple drawings. Over time they changed and have become more abstract, but one can still see the symbolic meaning represented by many of the kanji. The word Reiki is represented by two kanji, Rei and Ki. They are shown on the opposite page. Rei is the upper character and Ki is the lower character.

Rei – Spiritual Wisdom

The general meaning of Rei is universal and this is the definition many have used. However, Japanese ideograms have many levels of meaning. They vary from the mundane to the esoteric. So, while it is true that Rei can be interpreted as universal, meaning that it is present everywhere, there is a deeper understanding of this kanji, which for our use, is more meaningful in describing the healing art of Reiki.

As you can see, the kanji for Rei is composed of three sections. The upper section portrays clouds and it's meaning has to do with the heavens. In this case

the spiritual realms are represented and more specifically those higher areas of consciousness that are beyond ego. This area goes by various names such as spiritual consciousness, the Universal mind, God, the Supreme Being, the third heaven and so forth. It is out of these realms that creativity, genius, miraculous experiences, and spiritual healing originate. The lower section of Rei represents the earth and portrays layers of soil and stone. The middle section of the figure, which is composed of three rounded squares, represents three aspects of a human being—body, mind, and spirit. More specifically, this section represents the healer, who is located between heaven and earth and acts like a bridge to bring the wisdom, guidance, and healing of heaven down to the people and living things of the earth.

Ki - Life Energy

The word "Ki" means the same as *Chi* in Chinese, *Prana* in Sanskrit and *Ti* or *Ki* in Hawaiian; and science calls it *biofield energy*. It has been given many other names by various cultures.

Ki is life energy. It is also known as the vital life force or the universal life energy. This is the non-physical energy that animates all living things. As long as something is alive, it has life energy circulating through it and surrounding it; when it dies, the life energy departs. If your life energy is low, or if there is a restriction in its flow, you will be more vulnerable to illness. When it is high and flowing freely, you are less likely to get sick. Life energy plays an important role in everything we do. It animates the body and has higher levels of expression. Ki is also the primary energy of our emotions, thoughts, and spiritual life.

The kanji for Ki contains a cross with emanating lines. It is said that this part of the figure represents the steam above a pot of boiling rice. The steam represents the spiritual, life-enhancing properties of rice.

The Chinese place great importance on life energy, or Chi. They have studied it for thousands of years and have discovered there are many different kinds of Chi. The *Yellow Emperor's Classic of Internal Medicine*, which is over 4,000 years old, lists thirty-two different kinds of Chi or Ki.

The Japanese also think of Ki as having many ways it can express. Genki is original or healthy Ki, byoki is unhealty Ki, ki ga shimazu is disappointment, ki no hayai is excitment, ki ga omoi is depression, ki no okii is generosity and so on.

Ki is used by martial artists in their physical training and mental development. It is used in meditative breathing exercises called pranayama, and by the shamans of all cultures for divination, psychic awareness, manifestation, and healing. Ki is the non-physical energy used by all healers. Ki is present all around us and can be accumulated and guided by the mind. Russian researcher Semyon Kirlian developed a method in the 1940s for photographing the field of life energy that surrounds a person (see page 11). In fact Ki is thought to be the underlying energy of everything that exists.

Ki is influenced by the mind. If you have positive healthy thoughts, your Ki becomes stronger (genki). If you have unhealthy, negative thoughts, your Ki is weakened or becomes unhealthy (byoki).

Spiritually Guided Life Energy

Reiki is a special kind of Ki. It is Ki that is guided by spiritual consciousness, and is defined as spiritually guided life energy. This is a meaningful interpretation of the word Reiki. It more closely describes the experience most people have of it: Reiki guiding itself with its own wisdom, rather than requiring the direction of the practitioner.

Do All Healers Use Reiki?

There are many kinds of healing energy. All healing energy has Ki or life energy as one of its important parts. All healers use life energy or Ki, but not all use Reiki. Reiki is a special kind of healing energy that can only be channeled by someone who has been attuned to it. While it is possible that some people are born with Reiki or have gotten it some other way, most people need to receive a Reiki attunement to be able to use Reiki. Therefore, most healers who have not received the Reiki attunement from a Reiki Master are not using Reiki but another kind of healing energy.

Healers who have not taken a Reiki class can benefit from doing so. People who already do healing work report a consistent increase in the strength of their healing energies after taking Reiki training. This was verified for me when I first began teaching Reiki. Two clairvoyant healers I knew who had highly developed abilities decided to take Reiki training from me. They could easily see the life energy flowing through a person's body, as well as see the aura and chakras. They could communicate with a person's guides and Higher Self. They were adept at moving negative psychic energy out of the body as well as channeling healing energies. In my twenty years of metaphysical work, they were the most accurate and effective psychic healers I had met.

These healers later told me they had doubted there was anything I was teaching they couldn't already do, but they had taken the Reiki training simply to support me in my new work. After the attunement, they were amazed at the difference between the healing energies they had been using and Reiki. They said the Reiki energies were more powerful and of a much higher frequency. They also said Reiki didn't have to be guided like the other healing energies they used as the Reiki energy guided itself, flowing without the healer having to enter an altered state. They also said that the attunement process itself was a powerful healing experience for them, releasing restrictions relating to their healing work that they had unknowingly acquired as healers in past lives. They were very pleased they had taken the class.

The Attunement

Reiki is not taught in the way other healing techniques are taught. The ability to channel Reiki energy is transferred to the student by the Reiki Master during an attunement process. During the attunement, the Rei or spiritual consciousness makes adjustments in the student's chakras and energy pathways and also in deeper parts of one's consciousness to accommodate the ability to channel Reiki energy; it then links the student to the Reiki source. These changes are

unique for each person. The Reiki Master does not direct the process and is simply a channel for the attunement energy flowing from spiritual consciousness.

The Reiki attunement is a powerful spiritual experience and is the most important part of a Reiki class. The process is guided by Rei or spiritual consciousness, which fine tunes the experience for each student depending on what is needed. Some report having mystical experiences involving personal messages, healing, visions, and past-life experiences. The attunement can also increase psychic sensitivity. Students often report an opening of the third eye, increased intuitive awareness, or other psychic experiences after receiving a Reiki attunement. However, not everyone has these experiences. The meaningful experiences usually take place when the attunement energy works quickly and creates a rapid change in consciousness. However, for some students it's more appropriate for the attunement energy to work slowly over a long period of time which can sometimes extend even beyond the time when the attunement is being physically given by the teacher. Often when this happens, the experience isn't as dramatic and all that the student is aware of is a feeling of relaxation, even through the student is receiving all the benefits of the attunement. Because of this it's important to remember that what one experiences during the attunement isn't the main focus. Rather, it's the purpose of the attunement that is more important which is the new ability to channel Reiki energy. And this becomes apparent when the student begins to practice using Reiki on others. Remember also that to understand the value of one's Reiki energy, one must not only be aware of what is felt by the practitioner while giving a session, but more importantly what the client experiences. So be sure to check with the client about his or her experiences after beginning to use your new Reiki energy.

Once you have received a Reiki attunement, you will have Reiki for the remainder of your life; you can never lose it. While one attunement per level is all that is necessary to activate the ability to channel Reiki, additional attunements to levels already received have proven beneficial. These benefits include refinement of the Reiki energy one is channeling, increased strength of the energy, healing of personal problems, mental clarity, increased psychic sensitivity, and an expanded level of consciousness. At Reiki support groups offered by many Reiki teachers, additional attunements are often given at no extra charge.

A Cleansing Process

The Reiki attunement can start a cleansing process that affects the physical body as well as the mind and emotions. Toxins that have been stored in the body may be released along with feelings and thought patterns that are no longer useful. You could experience a headache, stomachache, weakness, or aches and pains. These are the effects of toxins being released from areas where they had been stored and is part of the process of releasing them from the body. Changes can also take place in the quality of your emotions and in your consciousness that indicate the release of emotional toxins. These experiences are actually a sign that healing is taking place. This does not always happen for everyone after a Reiki attunement, but when it does, it is important to understand what is happening so you can support its completion.

Whenever change takes place, even if it is good, a period of adjustment is necessary so that the body and various parts of your life can get used to the healthy new conditions. You may need more rest, and it can also be helpful to drink more water and to spend more time quietly contemplating your life and any changes you might need to make to support a healthier lifestyle. Many have found that a process of purification prior to and after the attunement improves the benefit one receives. Please refer to Appendix C for optional steps you can take to prepare for an attunement.

Giving Reiki

After the attunement, all that is necessary for practitioners to use Reiki is to place their hands on themselves or another with the intention of healing. The Reiki energies will begin flowing automatically.

It is not necessary to direct the Reiki energy. It has it's own awareness and intelligence and by connecting with the clients energy field will know how to work and what to do. The best results are achieved by simply remaining calm and relaxed and enjoying the soothing energies that are flowing through you. Note that while Reiki often goes to areas other than where one's hands are placed, it doesn't always do this. This is why it's important to use all the hand positions in a session and to follow the guidance you receive when using Byosen Scanning or Reiji-ho in determining where to place your hands.

Reiki Can Never Cause Harm

Because Reiki is guided by spiritual consciousness, it can never do harm. It always knows what a person needs and will adjust itself to create an effect that is appropriate. One never needs to worry about whether to give Reiki or not. It is always helpful and always safe. In addition, because the practitioner does not direct the healing and does not decide what to work on, or what to heal, the practitioner is not in danger of taking on the karma of the client. Because the practitioner is not doing the healing, it is also much easier for the ego to stay out of the way and allow the loving presence of spiritual consciousness to clearly shine through.

Reiki Never Depletes Your Energy

Because it is a channeled healing, the Reiki practitioner's energies are not part of the session and are never depleted. In fact, the Reiki consciousness considers both practitioner and client to be in need of healing so both receive benefit. Because of this, giving a session always increases one's energy and leaves one surrounded with loving feelings of well-being.

Anyone Can Learn Reiki

The ability to learn Reiki is not dependent on intellectual understanding, nor does one have to be able to meditate. It does not take years of practice. It is simply passed on through the teacher to the student during the attunement process. As soon as this happens, one has Reiki and can use it. Because of this, it is easily learned by anyone. Reiki is a pure form of healing not dependent on individual talent or efforts by the individual to acquire it. Because of this, the personality of the practitioner is less likely to cloud the significance of the experience. The feeling of being connected directly to God's healing love and protection is clearly apparent.

Self-Treatment

In addition to using Reiki on others, you can also treat yourself. This is one of the wonderful advantages of Reiki. It works just as well on you as it does on others. Complete instruction is given in the Reiki training for self-sessions. Chapter 7 shows the standard hand positions necessary to give yourself a complete Reiki session.

How Does Reiki Heal?

We are alive because life energy or Ki is flowing through us. Ki flows within the physical body through pathways called chakras, meridians, and nadis and can also be present and pass directly through the organs and tissues of the body. It also flows around us in a field of energy called the aura. The free and balanced flow of healthy Ki is the cause of well-being. It is Ki that animates the physical organs and tissues as it flows through them. Ki nourishes the organs and cells of the body, supporting them in their vital functions. When the flow of healthy Ki is disrupted, it causes diminished functioning within one or more of the organs and tissues of the physical body. Therefore, it is the disruption in the flow of healthy Ki that is the main cause of illness.

Ki is responsive to thoughts and feelings. When we have positive optimistic thoughts, we increase our flow of Ki and this causes us to feel better. However, when we have negative thoughts, our Ki is disrupted and diminished and we do not feel as good. When negative thoughts become lodged in the subconscious mind, they create a permanent disruption in the flow of healthy Ki. This happens when we either consciously or unconsciously accept negative thoughts or feelings about ourselves. These negative thoughts and feelings influence Ki and cause it to become byoki or unhealthy Ki. The byoki then attaches itself to the organs and tissues of the body and also disrupts the flow of healthy Ki. The organs and tissues of the body can be affected depending on the location of the blockage. This diminishes the vital function of those organs and cells of the physical body and unless the blockage is released, a person could eventually become ill.

When a person receives a Reiki session, the Rei or spiritually conscious part of the energy assesses where the person has byoki and then directs the healing energy, usually to the byoki that is nearest the hands. However, sometimes it will go to the byoki that is most in need of healing even if it is far from the hands. The Reiki energy then works with the negative thoughts and feelings that have created the byoki and are blocking one's flow of healthy Ki and replaces them with healthy thoughts and feelings thus releasing the byoki. This can

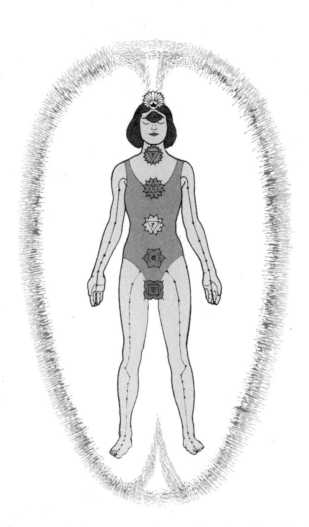

The human subtle energy system, showing the principle chakras and portions of the aura and meridian system.

happen in a number of ways. By flowing through the affected parts of the energy field and charging them with positive energy, Reiki raises the vibratory level in and around the physical body where the negative thoughts and feelings are attached. This causes the negative energy to break apart and fall away. In so doing, Reiki clears, straightens, and heals the energy pathways, thus allowing healthy Ki to flow in a natural way. Sometimes the entire field of blocking energy is lifted up to a higher level of consciousness where it is processed. Other times, it is melted away or burned up. When a block is released, sometimes a person will feel a cold sensation and when it is melted or burned up, a hot sensation. Once healthy Ki is flowing naturally, the physical organs and tissues are able to complete their healing process.

The Aura

The aura is a beautiful field of ever changing energy patterns that completely surrounds all living things. The oval shape surrounding the figure on the opposite page symbolizes the aura. However, the aura is actually composed of many layers starting with an inner layer closest to and often within the body and ending about 4–5 feet from the body. Even higher layers can exist further out than this. Each layer represents a different part of the persons consciousness with the inner layer connected to the physical body followed by higher layers associated with the emotional, mental, and spiritual levels of consciousness.

The aura is created by all of your thoughts and feelings, both conscious and unconscious as well as the energies flowing through the physical body. Your state of health is reflected in the aura as well as affected by the condition of

the aura and, in fact, many feel that the original cause of both illness and health is in the aura. Treating the aura with Reiki during Byosen Scanning can be an important part of a Reiki session.

It is possible to become aware of your own aura by doing various exercises. Use of the Reiki hand position on page 79 is one way to feel your aura. By energizing it with Reiki, your aura will become stronger, making it easier to feel. You can feel the auric field of others by using Byosen Scanning, which is explained on page 55. Byosen Scanning is also a way to treat the aura. Some people are so sensitive they can actually see the auric field and practitioners who can see the aura often use this information to improve the quality of their work.

The Chakras

The seven main chakras are represented by the flower shaped images on the front of the figure on the opposite page. The chakras are actually transformers of subtle energy. They take the Ki that is always around us and transform it into the various frequencies our subtle energy system needs to keep us healthy. The lowest or root chakra brings in the lower frequencies that are needed for physical survival and each higher chakra brings in higher energies such as those for healthy physical pleasure, expressing your will in the world, love of self and others, communication and creativity, with the highest or crown chakra bringing in the spiritual levels of energy. Each chakra corresponds with a layer of the aura. Negative feelings or thoughts can become lodged in the chakras reducing the amount of subtle energy they are able to provide and adversely affecting one's health.

Although it was not a part of the original style of Reiki practiced by Usui Sensei, Haysashi Sensei or Takata Sensei, treating the chakras can also be an optional part of giving a Reiki session.

The Meridians

The meridians are pathways through which the subtle energy flows within the physical body. The meridians contain energy points generally referred to as acupuncture or acupressure points. Each meridian is usually associated with an organ or physical system of the body and supplies that organ or system with specific kinds of Ki. As an example, the liver meridian starts on the top of the foot and travels up the leg and to the liver.

What Can Be Treated?

Reiki is both powerful and gentle. In its long history of use it has aided in helping to heal virtually every known illness and injury including life threatening problems like multiple sclerosis, heart disease, and cancer as well as skin problems, cuts, bruises, broken bones, headaches, colds, flu, sore throat, sunburn, fatigue, insomnia, and impotence. It is always beneficial and works to improve the effectiveness of all other types of therapy. A session feels like a wonderful, glowing radiance and has many benefits for both client and practitioner, including positive states of consciousness and spiritual experiences.

Reiki Works with Medical Care

Reiki works in harmony with all other kinds of treatment including medical and psychological care. In fact, Reiki is offered as part of regular patient care in over 800 hospitals across the U.S. including being given in operating rooms and intensive care units.[1] According to a series of interviews I did with nurses and other medical professionals who practice Reiki in hospitals, Reiki decreases recovery time from surgery, improves mental attitude, and reduces unwanted side effects of medications including chemotherapy, radiation, and other medical procedures.[2] A research study at Hartford Hospital in Hartford, Connecticut indicates that Reiki improved patient sleep by 86 percent, reduced pain by 78 percent, reduced nausea by 80 percent, and reduced anxiety during pregnancy by 94 percent.[3]

Reiki has also been used in conjunction with psychotherapy to improve the healing of emotional trauma and other issues. Its psychological benefits can include improved memory and greater self-confidence. Use in psychology is usually done in a hands-off method, often from across the room. If clients have a physical or psychological condition and want to be treated with Reiki, it is recommended that they do so under the supervision of an enlightened medical doctor, psychologist, or other licensed health care professional.

[1] For a list of hospitals that offer Reiki sessions to their patients, that also includes a detailed description of their Reiki programs, see www.centerforreikiresearch. org, and click on Hospital List.

[2] William Lee Rand, "Reiki in Hospitals," *Reiki Newsletter* (Winter 1997), precursor to *Reiki News Magazine*; see also www.centerforreikiresearch.org/ Articles_ReikiInHosp.aspx.

[3] Hartford Hospital, Integrative Medicine, Outcomes, www.harthosp.org/integrativemed/outcomes/default. aspx#outcome6. Measurements cited were obtained during the initial pilot phase of the study, December 1999-December 2000.

Is Reiki a Religion?

While Reiki is spiritual in nature in that it provides love and compassion to the client, it is not a religion. It has no dogma and does not conflict with religious belief. People who are followers of all the various religions have practiced Reiki and find that it enhances their religious experience. For answers to questions Christians might have about the practice of Reiki, please go to www.christianreiki.org

Kirlian Photography

Kirlian photography is a technique of photographing the etheric energy patterns around living things. Pioneered by Russian researcher Semyon Kirlian during the 1940s, it is based on a phenomenon known as corona discharge. When an object is in a high-frequency electrical field and becomes grounded, a spark discharges between the object and the electrode. A piece of film is placed between the object and the electrode and the discharge pattern is captured on the film. When a living thing is used as the object, beautiful colors and patterns are created on the film. This discharge pattern seems to follow the pattern of the etheric aura.

Reiki Photograph

The Kirlian photograph below was taken in May 1990 by Doris Kangas. Doris asked me to be a subject for the Kirlian process to determine if Reiki energy could be detected. Her process involves taking fingerprint Kirlian photos with a Polaroid film device inside a black bag. Three sets of fingertip photos were taken on the same film. The first three fingers of my right hand were used. During the first two photos I just sat calmly. During the last photo, which is the set of prints at the bottom, I placed my left hand on my leg and asked Reiki to flow. When I felt a strong flow of Reiki in my right hand, I told Doris I was ready and she took the picture. Doris has taken hundreds of Kirlian photos and this was the first time she took one that looked like this. It shows Reiki energy emanating from the palm chakra. One beam can be seen to emerge between the thumb and forefinger, and the main beam between the forefinger and middle finger. In the original color photo, the beams are white in the middle, turning blue/white on the edges and indigo at the bottom.

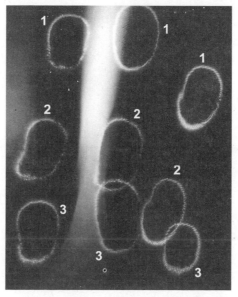

Kirlian photo of Reiki energy

Notes

Chapter 2
History of Reiki

Mrs. Hawayo Takata (Takata Sensei) brought Reiki from Japan to the West in 1937 and continued to practice and teach until her passing in 1980. Because of her devotion, Reiki has been passed on to millions of people all over the world, and the numbers continue to grow! And as you will see, if it wasn't for her, Reiki most likely would never have been discovered by the West and even in Japan would have been practiced secretly by only a small number of people.

Until the 1990s, the only information we had about Reiki came from Takata Sensei. Her story of Reiki was recorded on tape, and this recording is still available along with a transcript of the contents.[1] In the past most people including many authors simply accepted Takata Sensei's interpretation of the history of Reiki as accurate without attempting to do any additional research. Because of this, her version of the story was repeated in all the earlier books written on Reiki. (Fortunately many current authors are using more recent historical information.)

In the course of researching the origins of Reiki, I learned that Takata Sensei took liberties with the history of its development. In 1990, for example, I wrote to Doshisha University in Kyoto, Japan where Takata Sensei reported that the founder of Reiki, Usui Sensei, had held the office of president. I had hoped to gain additional information that would help us understand who Usui Sensei really was. I also contacted the University of Chicago, from which Usui Sensei had obtained a degree according to Takata Sensei. Neither university had ever heard of him.[2] This disappointing discovery led me to wonder if other parts of the Takata Sensei version of Reiki were also inaccurate. In talking with several early Reiki Masters about this discovery, I was told that Takata Sensei had westernized the story of Reiki by changing certain details and adding others to make it more appealing to Americans.

I continued to seek additional information about the history of Reiki, but attempts to secure it went slowly at first. The main reason for this is that after World War II, the U.S. government had complete control over Japan for a time and banned all Eastern healing methods in Japan and required that only Western medicine be practiced there. The members of the organization Usui Sensei started, the *Usui Reiki Ryoho Gakkai*, decided they wanted to find a way to continue to practice Reiki. Some of the other healing groups such as the Acupuncturists were able to get a license to practice, but the Gakkai chose not to go through this process. In order to continue to practice Reiki, they decided to become a secret society and practice only among themselves and not talk about Reiki to anyone outside their organization.[3] This made it difficult for anyone to learn about Reiki including the Japanese. In fact, if someone in Japan wanted to learn Reiki after the war, he or she had to travel to the U.S. to learn or had to learn from a Western trained Reiki teacher who traveled to Japan. Because of this, even now most Reiki practiced in Japan is a combination of Western and Japanese Reiki.

---

[1] *Mrs. Takata Speaks, The History of Reiki*, (Southfield, MI: Vision Publications, 1979).

[2] See http://www.reiki.org/Download/TakataLettersAnd Documents.pdf

[3] Tadao Yamaguchi, *Light on the Origins of Reiki* (Twin Lakes, WI: Lotus Press, 2007), p. 66.

This is why an accurate history of Reiki took so long to unfold up to that point in time. Then in 1996, I received from Japan a copy of the Original Reiki Ideals, which were different and more expansive than what had been presented by Mrs. Takata. They included the idea that chanting and offering prayers are important to Reiki practice.[4] In 1997, Arjava Petter's book, *Reiki Fire* was published, which was the first of a series of books on Japanese Reiki. He along with his wife, Chetna Kobayashi, had made contact with the Gakkai. They had discovered the location of Usui Sensei's grave and many other facts including information on the Japanese Reiki Techniques, all of which were revealed in his books and subsequent workshops.

Invited by Arjava Petter, Laura Gifford (now Laurelle Gaia) and I went to Japan in 1997, and with Arjava as our guide, we were taken to Usui Sensei's grave and Mt. Kurama and much of the new information was explained to us.[5]

---

[4] Toshitaka Mochizuki, *Iyashi No Te* [Healing Hands] (1995), p. 227, ISBN 4-88481-420-7 C0011 P1400E; "The Original Reiki Ideals," *Reiki News* (Fall 1996); and page vi of this manual. To order the Original Reiki Ideals: www.reikiwebstore.com.

[5] For more information, see Appendix A, "Discovering the Roots of Reiki," and The Inscription on the Usui Memorial section below.

Usui Memorial Stone

In 1999 and 2000 I invited Arjava and Chetna to come to teach workshops on the Japanese Reiki Techniques across the United States. In addition, in November, 2001, I took Reiki I&II from Chiyoko Yamaguchi in Japan, a Shihan (Reiki Master) who received her training from Hayashi Sensei. (She passed on in 2003). In October 2002 I took Gendai Reiki training from Hiroshi Doi—who is a member of the *Usui Reiki Ryoho Gakkai*—and also had two detailed interviews with him.[6] It is from these sources and my continued contact with these and other Reiki researchers that my understanding of the history of Reiki along with how Usui Sensei and Hayashi Sensei taught and practiced Reiki has developed.

A More Accurate History of Reiki

The following is an updated history of Reiki based on accurate, verifiable information. Where possible, sources have been referenced so others can follow up on this research if desired. The history begins with a look at the inscription on the memorial stone that was erected in 1927 in memory of Mikao Usui Sensei, founder of the Reiki healing system.

The Inscription on the Usui Memorial

The inscription on the Usui Memorial, dating from 1927, was written by Juzaburo Ushida, a Shihan who was trained by Usui Sensei and able to teach and practice Reiki the same way he did.[7] He also

succeeded Usui Sensei as president of the Usui Reiki Ryoho Gakkai. Masayuki Okata, also a member of the Usui Reiki Ryoho Gakkai, was the editor. The English translation was done by Tetsuyuki Ono and is reprinted here from the book, *Iyashino Gendai Reiki- ho*, with permission from the author, Hiroshi Doi.

The large kanji at the top of the memorial stone reads: "Memorial of Usui Sensei's Virtue." The remainder of the inscription reads as follows:

What you can naturally realize through cultivation and training is called "VIRTUE" and it is called "MERIT" to spread a method of leadership and relief and practice it. It is people of many merits and a good deal of virtue that can be eventually called a great founder. People who started a new learning and founded a fresh sect among sages, philosophers, geniuses etc., named from the ancient times, were all those as mentioned above. We can say that Usui-Sensei is also one of those people.

He started newly a method to improve body and spirit based on REIKI in the universe. Hearing of the rumor, people who would like to learn the treatment and undergo the cure gathered from all quarters all at once. Really, it was very busy indeed.

Usui-Sensei, whose popular name is Mikao and whose pen name is Gyohan, came from Taniai-village, Yamagata- district, Cifu Prefecture, and had forefathers named Tsunetane Chiba who had played an active part as a military commander between the end of Heian Period and the beginning of Kamakura Period (1180-1230). His father's real name is Taneuji and his

---

[6] William Lee Rand, "An Interview with Hiroshi Doi," *Reiki News Magazine*, Pts. 1 and 2 (Summer 2003), 9-11; (Fall 2003), p. 12-14.

[7] Tadao Yamaguchi. "Excerpts from Light on the Origin of Reiki" *Reiki News Magazine* (Spring 2011), p. 19. Included in this article is a photo of the 20 shihan taught by Usui Sensei. The text below the photo indicates that these are the students of Usui Sensei who are authorized to teach in the same way he taught. Juzaburo Ushida is in the photo.

popular name is Uzaemon. His mother came and got married from the family named Kawai.

Usui-Sensei was born on 15th August, 1865. Having learned under difficulties in his childhood, he studied hard with efforts and he was by far superior in ability to his friends.

After growing up, he went over to Europe and America, and also studied in China. In spite of his real ability, however, he was not always successful in life. Although he was compelled to lead an unfortunate and poor life so often, he strove much more than before to harden his body and mind without flinching from the difficulties.

One day, Usui-Sensei climbed Mt. Kurama, where he began to do penance while fasting. Suddenly on the twenty first day from the start, he felt a great REIKI over his head, and at the same time as he was spiritually awakened he acquired the REIKI cure. When he tried it on his own body and members' of his family also, it brought an immediate result on them.

Having said "It is much better to give this power widely to a lot of people in the world and enjoy it among them than to keep it exclusively by his family members," Usui-Sensei moved his dwelling to Aoyama Harajuku, Tokyo in April, 1922 and established an institute, where the REIKI cure was instructed openly to the public and the treatment was given, too. People came there from far and near to ask for his guidance and cure, and they over-flowed outside, making a long line.

Tokyo had a very big fire caused by a great earthquake in Kanto district in September, 1923, when the injured and sick persons suffered from pains everywhere. Usui-Sensei felt a deep anxiety about that, and he was engaged in a cure, going around inside the city every day. We can hardly calculate how many persons were saved from death with his devotion. His activities of relief, in which he extended his hands of love over to those suffering people against this emergent situation, can be outlined as noted above.

Thereafter, his training center became too small to receive the visitors, so he built a new house in Nakano outside the city in February 1925 and transferred there. As his reputation got higher and higher, it was so often when he received an offer of engagement from everywhere throughout the nation. In accordance with these requests he traveled to Kure and Hiroshima, then entered Saga and reached Fukuyama. It was at the inn at which he stayed on his way that he caught a disease abruptly, and he passed away at the age of sixty-two.

His wife got married, coming from the Suzuki family, and she is named Sadako and has a son and a daughter. The son's name is Fuji, and he succeeds to the Usui family.

Usui-Sensei's natural character was gentle and prudent, and he did not keep up appearances. His body was big and sturdy, and his face was always beaming with a smile. But when he faced the difficulties he went ahead with a definite will and yet persevered well, keeping extremely careful. He was a man of versatile talents and also a book lover, knowing well in the wide range from history, biography, medical science, canons of Christianity and Buddhism and psychology up to magic of fairyland, art of curse, science of divination and physiognomy.

In my opinion, it is evident to everybody that Usui-Sensei's cultivation

& training were based on his career of art and science, and the cultivation & training became a clue to create the REIKI cure.

Reviewing the fact, I understand what the REIKI cure is aiming at is not only to heal the diseases but also to correct the mind by virtue of a God-sent spiritual ability, keep the body healthy and enjoy a welfare of life. In teaching the persons, therefore, we are supposed to first let them realize the last instructions of the Emperor Meiji, and chant the 5 admonitions morning and evening to keep them in mind.

The 5 admonitions in question are:

1. Don't get angry today.
2. Don't be grievous.
3. Express your thanks.
4. Be diligent in your business.
5. Be kind to others.

These are really the important precepts for a cultivation, just the same as those by which the ancient sages admonished themselves. Usui-Sensei emphasized that 'This is surely a secret process to bring a good fortune and also a miraculous medicine to remedy all kinds of diseases,' by which he made his purpose of teaching clear and accurate. Furthermore, he tried to aim at making his way of guidance as easy and simple as possible, so nothing is difficult to understand therein. Every time when you sit quietly and join your hands to pray and chant morning and evening, you can develop a pure and sound mind, and there is just an essence in making the most of that for your daily life. This is the reason why the REIKI cure can very easily spread over anybody.

The phase of life is very changeable in these days, and people's thoughts

Mikao Usui
(Usui Sensei), founder of
the Reiki System of Healing

are apt to change, too. Could we fortunately succeed in spreading the REIKI cure everywhere, we feel sure that it would have to be very helpful in order to prevent people from disordering their moral sense. It never extends people anything but the benefits of healing long term illness, chronic disease and bad habit.

The number of pupils who learned from Usui-Sensei amounts to more than 2000 persons. Some leading pupils living in Tokyo among them gather at the training center and take over his work, while other pupils in the country also do everything to popularize the REIKI cure. Although our teacher already passed away, we have to do the very best to hand the REIKI cure down to the public forever and spread it much more. Ah! What a great thing he did; to have *unsparingly given people what he had felt and realized by himself!*

As a result of our pupils' recent meeting and discussion, we decided to erect a stone monument at the graveyard in his family temple so that we may bring his virtuous deed to light and transmit it to posterity; so, I was requested to arrange an epitaph for the monument. As I was much impressed by his great meritorious deed and also struck by our pupils' warm hearts of making much of the bond between master and pupil, I dared not refuse the request, but described the outline.

Therefore, I do expect heartily that people in the future generations would not forget to look up at the monument in open-eyed wonder.

—Usuida, in February, 1927. Edited by Masayuki Okada, The Junior 3rd Rank, the 3rd Order of Merit, Doctor of Literature. Written by Juzaburo Usuhida, The Junior 4th Class of Services, Rear Admiral.

Mikao Usui

Mikao Usui, or Usui Sensei as he is called by Reiki students in Japan, was born August 15, 1865 in the village of Taniai in the Yamagata district of Gifu prefecture, which is located near present-day Nagoya, Japan.[8]

He had an avid interest in learning and worked hard at his studies. As he grew older, he traveled to Europe and China to further his education. His curriculum included medicine, psychology and religion as well as the art of divination, which Asians have long considered to be a worthy skill.[9] Usui Sensei also became a member of the Rei Jyutu Ka, a metaphysical group dedicated to developing psychic abilities.[10] He had many jobs including civil servant, company employee and journalist, and he helped rehabilitate prisoners.[11] Eventually he became the secretary to Shinpei Goto, head of the department of health and welfare who later became the mayor of Tokyo. The connections Usui Sensei made at this job helped him to also become a successful businessman.[12]

The depth and breadth of his experiences inspired him to direct his attention toward discovering the purpose of life. In his search he came across the description of a special state of consciousness that once achieved would not only provide an understanding of one's life purpose, but would also guide one to achieve it. This special state is called An-shin Ritus-mei (pronounced on sheen dit sue may). In this special state, one is always at peace regardless of what is taking place in the outer world. And it is from this place of peace that one completes one's life purpose. One of the special features of this state is that it maintains itself without any effort on the part of the individual; the experience of peace simply wells up spontaneously from within and is a type of enlightenment.

Usui Sensei understood this concept on an intellectual level and dedicated his life to achieving it; this is considered to be an important step on Usui Sensei's spiritual path. He discovered that one

8 Inscription on Usui Memorial, Saihoji Temple, Suginami, Tokyo, Japan.

9 Inscription on Usui Memorial.

10 Mochizuki, Iyashi No Te. See note 3.

11 Yamaguchi, *Light on the Origins of Reiki*, p. 61.

12 "Searching the Roots of Reiki," *The Twilight Zone* (April 1986),: p. 140-143. This article can be viewed on the web at http://www.pwpm.com/threshold/origins2.html. (Note that this Japanese magazine is no longer in business.)

path to An-shin Ritsu-mei is through the practice of Zazen meditation. So he found a Zen teacher who accepted him as a student and began to practice Zazen. After three years practice, he had not been successful and sought further guidance. His teacher suggested a more severe practice in which the student must be willing to die in order to achieve An-shin Ritsu-meiwhich.[13,14]

So with this in mind he prepared for death and in February, 1922, he went to Mt. Kurama to fast and meditate until he passed to the next world. In addition, we know there is a small waterfall on Mt. Kurama where even today people go to meditate. This meditation involves standing under the waterfall and allowing the water to strike and flow over the top of the head, a practice that is said to activate the crown chakra. Japanese Reiki Masters think that Usui Sensei may have used this meditation as part of his practice. In any case, as time passed he became weaker and weaker. It was now March, 1922 and at midnight of the twenty-first day, a powerful light suddenly entered his mind through the top of his head and he felt as if he had been struck by lightning; this caused him to fall unconscious.

As the sun rose, he awoke and realized that whereas before he had felt very weak and near death, he was now filled with an extremely enjoyable state of vitality that he had never experienced before; a miraculous type of high frequency spiritual energy had displaced his normal consciousness and replaced it with an amazingly new level of awareness. He experienced himself as being the energy and consciousness of the Universe and that the special state of enlightenment he had sought had been given to him as a gift. He was overjoyed by this realization.

When this happened, he was filled with excitement and went running down the mountain. On his way down he stubbed his toe on a rock and fell down. And in the same way anyone would do, he placed his hands over the toe, which was in pain. As he did this, healing energy began flowing from his hands all by itself. The pain in his toe went away and the toe was healed. Usui Sensei was amazed by this. He realized that in addition to the illuminating experience he had received, he had also received the gift of healing.[15]

Usui Sensei practiced this new ability with his family and developed his healing system through experimentation and by using skills and information based on his previous study of religious practices, philosophy and spiritual disciplines. He called his system of healing Shin-Shin Kai-Zen Usui Reiki Ryo-Ho (The Usui Reiki Treatment Method for Improvement of Body and Mind)[16] or in its simplified form Usui Reiki Ryoho (Usui Reiki Healing Method). It is important to know that Usui Sensei didn't create Reiki as there were other methods of Reiki healing in Japan prior to Usui Sensei creating his method and in fact one was called Reiki Ryoho.[17]

---

[13] Frank Arjava Petter, *This is Reiki: Transformation of Body, Mind and Soul, From the Origins to the Practice* (Twin Lakes: WI: Lotus Press) p. 44.

[14] In an alternate version of this story it is said that Usui Sensei's personal life and business had failed and that he had gone to Mt. Kurama to meditate to gain clarity on what to do to solve his problems. See Takai, "Searching the Roots of Reiki," p. 140-143.

[15] Doi, *Iyashino Gendai Reiki-ho, Modern Reiki Method of Healing,* p. 35. This story has been passed down within the Usui Reiki Ryoho Gakkai. According to Doi, it is also written in "Kaiin no tame no Reiki Ryoho no Shiori" (Guide of Reiki Ryoho for the members), September 1, 1974.

[16] This is based on the translation of an original document written by Usui Sensei. See: http://www.reiki.org/japanesetechniques/5principles.html

[17] William Lee Rand, "Reiki Before Usui," *Reiki News Magazine* (Spring 2014), p. 32-33.

In April 1922, he moved to Tokyo and started a healing society that he named Usui Reiki Ryoho Gakkai (Usui Reiki Healing Method Society). He also opened a Reiki clinic in Harajuku, Aoyama, Tokyo. There he taught classes and gave treatments.[18]

The first degree of his training was called Shoden (First Degree) and was divided into four levels: Loku-Tou, Go-Tou, Yon-Tou, and San-Tou. (Note that when Takata Sensei taught this level, which in the West we refer to as Reiki Level I, she combined all four levels into one. This is most likely why she did four attunements for Level I.) The next degree was called Okuden (Inner Teaching) and had two levels: Okuden-Zen-ki (first part), and Okuden-Koe-ki (second part). The next degree was called Shinpiden (Mystery Teaching), which is what Western Reiki calls Master level. The Shinpiden level includes, Shihan-Kaku (assistant teacher) and Shihan (venerable teacher).[19]

Contrary to previous understanding, Usui Sensei had only three symbols, the same three we use in the West in Reiki II. He did not use a master symbol. This fact has been verified by Hiroshi Doi and by research done by Hyakuten Inamoto, Arjava Petter and Tadao Yamaguchi.[20]

In 1923, the great Kanto earthquake devastated Tokyo. More than 140,000 people died and over half of the houses and buildings were shaken down or burned. An overwhelming number of people were left homeless, injured, sick and grieving.[21] Usui Sensei felt great compassion for the people and began treating as many as he could with Reiki. This was a tremendous amount of work, and it was at this time that he began training other Shihan (teachers) so that they could help him more quickly train others to be Reiki practitioners and help the sick and injured. It was also at this time that he further developed his system of Reiki, including adding the three symbols and devising a more formal Reiju (attunement) process.[22]

The Reiju process was different than the method used now in that Usui Sensei had just one type of Reiju that was given over and over. He didn't have a different Reiju for each level and there was no Reiju to activate the symbols. It was taught that it is important for the student to get as many Reiju as possible as this was an important way to increase and refine the quality of one's Reiki energy.[23]

Demand for Reiki became so great that he outgrew his clinic, so in 1925 he built a bigger one in Nakano, Tokyo. Because of this, Usui Sensei's reputation as a healer spread all over Japan. He began to travel so he could teach and treat more people. During his travels across Japan he directly taught more than 2,000 students and initiated twenty Shihan,[24] each being given the same

[18] Yamaguchi, Light on the Origins of Reiki, p. 63-64.

[19] Walter Lubeck, Frank Arjava Petter, William Lee Rand, The Spirit of Reiki (Twin Lakes, WI: Lotus Press, 2003).

[20] William Lee Rand, "Interview with Hiroshi Doi, Part I," Reiki News Magazine (Spring 2014) p. 27. Frank Arjava Petter, This is Reiki (Twin Lakes, WI: Lotus Press, 2012), p. 174

[21] "Earthquakes Tokyo-Yokohama," Encyclopedia Britannica (1997), CD-ROM.

[22] Frank Arjava Petter, Reiki Darma Newsletter Number 31, January 1, 2011

[23] William Lee Rand, "An Interview with Doi Sensei," Reiki News Magazine (Spring 2014), p. 27.

[24] Go to Reiki News Magazine (Spring 2011), p. 18 for a photo of Usui Sensei and the twenty Shihan. Note that while all in the photo were authorized to give Reiju, some were not Shinpiden. In those days some of the centers did not have a Shinpiden to give Reiju so Reiju was taught to the leader of the center.

understanding of Reiki and approved to teach and give Reiju in the same way he did.[25]

The Japanese government issued him a *Kun San To* award for doing honorable work to help others.[26] While traveling to Fukuyama to teach, he suffered a stroke and died March 9, 1926.[27] His grave is at Saihoji Temple, in Suginami, Tokyo, although some claim that his ashes are located elsewhere.

After Usui Sensei died, his students erected a memorial stone next to his gravestone. (See page 14.) Mr. J. Ushida, a Shihan trained by Usui Sensei, took over as president of the Usui Reiki Ryoho Gakkai, and was responsible for creating and erecting the Usui Memorial stone and ensuring that the gravesite would be maintained. Mr. Ushida was followed by Mr. Ilichi Taketomi, Mr. Yoshiharu Watanabe, Mr. Toyoichi Wanami and Ms. Kimiko Koyama. The current successor to Usui Sensei is Mr. Mahayoshi Kondo, who became president in 1998.

Contrary to what we have been told in the West, there is no "lineage bearer" or "Grand Master" of the organization started by Usui Sensei—only the succession of presidents listed above.[28] Among the twenty teachers initiated by Usui Sensei are Toshihiro Eguchi, Jusaburo Guida, Kan'ichi Taketomi, Toyoichi Wanami, Yoshiharu Watanabe, Keizo Ogawa, J. Ushida, and Chujiro Hayashi.[29] Contrary to one version of the Reiki story, Chujiro Hayashi was not the Gakkai's successor to Usui Sensei,

but rather Mr. J. Ushida as previously mentioned. It is also important to note that the first four presidents of the Gakkai who followed Usui Sensei were Shihan who had been trained directly by Usui Sensei, thus assuring that the Gakkai understanding, practice and teaching methods were the same as that of Usui Sensei.

Chujiro Hayashi

Before his passing, Usui Sensei had asked Hayashi Sensei to open his own Reiki clinic and to expand and develop Reiki Ryoho based on his previous experience as a medical doctor in the Navy. Motivated by this request, Hayashi Sensei started a school and clinic called

Chujiro Hayashi

Hayashi Reiki Kenkyukai (Institute). After Usui Sensei's passing he left the Gakkai.[30] At his clinic he kept careful records of

[25] Yamaguchi, *Light on the Origins of Reiki*, p. 63-64.

[26] Takai, *The Twilight Zone*, p. 140-143.

[27] Inscription on Usui Memorial.

[28] Frank Arjava Petter, *Reiki Fire*, (Twin Lakes, WI: Lotus Light, 1997), p. 26. ISBN 0-914955-50-0.

[29] This list comes from the research of Frank Arjava Petter.

[30] William Lee Rand, "An Interview with Hiroshi Doi, Part II," Reiki News Magazine, (Fall 2003), p. 13.

all the illnesses and conditions patients who came to see him had. He also kept records of which Reiki hand positions worked best to treat each patient. Based on these records he created the *Reiki Ryoho Shinshin* (Guidelines for Reiki Healing Method).[31] This healing guide was part of a class manual he gave to his students. Many of his students received their Reiki training in return for working in his clinic.[32]

Hayashi Sensei also changed the way Reiki sessions are given. Rather than have the client seated in a chair and treated by one practitioner as Usui Sensei had done, Hayashi Sensei had the client lie on a treatment table and receive treatment from several practitioners at a time. He also created a new more effective system for giving Reiju (attunements).[33] In addition, he developed a new method of teaching Reiki that he used when he traveled. In this method, he taught both Shoden and Okuden (Reiki I&II) together in one five-day seminar. Each day included two to three hours of instruction and one Reiju.[34]

Because of his trip to Hawaii in 1937–38 prior to the Japanese attack on Pearl Harbor, he was asked by the Japanese military to provide information about the location of warehouses and other military targets in Honolulu. He refused to do so and was declared a traitor. This caused him to "lose face," which meant he and his family would be disgraced and would be ostracized from Japanese society. The only solution was seppuku (ritual suicide), which he carried out. He died honorably on May 11, 1940.[35]

Hawayo Takata

The following is a summary of Mrs. Hawayo Takata's version of her early years leading up to her contact with Reiki at the Hayashi clinic:

Hawayo Takata

She stated that she was born on December 24th, 1900, on the island of Kauai, Hawaii. Her parents were Japanese immigrants and her father worked in the sugar cane fields. She eventually married the bookkeeper of the plantation where she was employed. His name was Saichi Takata and they had two daughters. In October 1930 Saichi died at the age of 34, leaving Mrs. Takata to raise their two children.

---

[31] A translation of this healing guide can be found on p. 63.

[32] Frank Arjava Petter interviewing Tsutomo Oishi, a member of Usui Reiki Ryoho Gakkai.

[33] Rand, "An Interview with Hiroshi Doi, Part II," *Reiki News Magazine*, (Fall 2003), p. 12.

[34] Yamaguchi, *Light on the Origins of Reiki*, p. 28.

[35] Ibid., p. 69.

In order to provide for her family, she had to work very hard with little rest. After five years she developed severe abdominal pain and a lung condition, and she had a nervous breakdown. Soon after this one of her sisters died and it was Mrs. Takata's responsibility to travel to Japan, where her parents had resettled to deliver the news. She also felt she could receive help for her health in Japan.

After informing her parents, she entered a hospital and stated that she was diagnosed with a tumor, gallstones, appendicitis and asthma.[36] She was told to prepare for an operation but opted to visit Hayashi Sensei's clinic instead.

Mrs. Takata was unfamiliar with Reiki but was impressed that the diagnosis of Reiki practitioners at the clinic closely matched the doctor's at the hospital. She began receiving treatments. Two Reiki practitioners would treat her each day. The heat from their hands was so strong, she said, that she thought they were secretly using some kind of equipment. Seeing the large sleeves of the Japanese kimono worn by one, she thought she had found the secret place of concealment. Grabbing his sleeves one day she startled the practitioner, but, of course, found nothing. When she explained what she was doing, he began to laugh and then told her about Reiki and how it worked.

Mrs. Takata got progressively better and in four months was completely healed. She wanted to learn Reiki for herself. In the spring of 1936 she received First Degree Reiki from Dr. Hayashi. She then worked with him for a year and received Second Degree Reiki. Mrs. Takata returned to Hawaii in 1937, followed shortly thereafter by Hayashi

Sensei and his daughter who came to help establish Reiki there. In February of 1938 Hayashi Sensei initiated Hawayo Takata as a Reiki Master.

To summarize Takata Sensei's Reiki background, she traveled from Hawaii to Japan to tell her parents about the death of her sister. Having been diagnosed with several ailments, the main one being asthma, she was guided to Hayashi Sensei's clinic in Tokyo and after receiving four months of Reiki treatments was completely cured.[37] She wanted to learn Reiki in order to continue treating herself and also to take it back to Hawaii to share with others. Hayashi Sensei allowed her to work at his clinic and also began giving her Reiki training. She worked one year at the clinic and eventually received the *Shinpiden* level (Reiki Master). Hayashi Sensei officially acknowledged this in Hawaii on February 21, 1938, and also stated that she was one of thirteen Reiki Masters trained by him.[38]

Takata Sensei practiced Reiki in Hawaii, establishing several clinics, one of which was located in Hilo on the Big Island. She gave treatments and initiated students up to Reiki II. She became a well-known healer and traveled to the U.S. mainland and other parts of the world teaching and giving treatments. She was a powerful healer who attributed her success to the fact that she did a lot of Reiki on each client. She would often do multiple treatments, each sometimes lasting hours, and she often initiated members of a client's family so they could give Reiki to the client as well.

[36] Vera Graham, "Mrs. Takata Opens Minds to Reiki," *The (San Mateo) Times*, May 17, 1975.

[37] Patsy Matsura, "Mrs. Takata and Reiki Power," *Honolulu Advertiser*, Feb. 25, 1974.

[38] This information was recorded on Mrs. Takata's Reiki certificate and in Mrs. Takata's handwritten notes dated May 1936. A copy of her Reiki certificate is included in the article "How Hawayo Takata Practiced and Taught Reiki" located on page 157.

It was not until after 1970 that Takata Sensei began initiating Reiki Masters. She charged a fee of $10,000 for Mastership even though the training took only a weekend.[39] This high fee was not part of the Usui system, and she may have charged this fee as her way of creating a feeling of respect for Reiki. She said that one should never do treatments or provide training for free, but should always charge a fee or get something in return. She also said that one must study with just one Reiki teacher and stay with that teacher the rest of one's life.[40] In addition, she said that she did not provide written instruction or allow her students to take notes or to tape record the classes and students were not allowed to make any written copies of the Reiki symbols. She said that this was because Reiki is an oral tradition and that everything had to be memorized.[41] While this is generally true, she didn't always teach the same way and in at least one class she allowed her students to take notes and gave them handouts.[42]

It is not certain why she said Reiki is an oral tradition or why she taught Reiki this way. What we do know from our research in Japan and the research of others is that these rules are not part of the way Usui Sensei or Hayashi Sensei practiced Reiki. In fact, Takata Sensei received a Reiki manual from Hayashi Sensei indicating that the oral tradition was not how Hayashi Sensei

taught.[43] In addition, Takata Sensei taught Reiki differently from how she had been taught. She simplified and standardized the hand positions so that every treatment would be the same. She called this the "foundation treatment," containing just eight hand positions.[44] She also eliminated the Japanese Reiki Techniques.

It is also likely that she is the one who changed the attunement process by creating a different attunement for each level, indicated that the attunement empowered the symbols and added the Master symbol, as these features were not taught by either Usui Sensei or Hayashi Sensei.[45]

Before Mrs. Takata made her transition on December 11, 1980, she had initiated twenty-two Reiki Masters.[46] These twenty-two Masters began teaching others. However, Mrs. Takata had made each one take a sacred oath to teach Reiki exactly as she had taught. This made it difficult for most of them to change, even though some of her rules made it more difficult to learn, which seemed to go against the nature of Reiki.

This version of the history of Reiki from Usui Sensei to Mrs. Takata relies on verifiable

---

[39] Bethel Phaigh, "Journey into Consciousness," 130. Other Masters initiated by Mrs. Takata have confirmed that she gave Reiki Master training in a weekend.

[40] We know that Keizo Ogawa took Reiki Master training from Usui Sensei and Kan'ichi Taketomi, so it is not likely this rule came from Usui Sensei.

[41] "Mrs. Takata Speaks." See footnote 1. This was also explained to me by Bethal Phaigh in 1981 when I took Reiki I from her.

[42] William Lee Rand, "Takata's Handouts," *Reiki News Magazine* (Summer 2009): 58. This article contains the handouts and notes taken during one of her classes.

[43] A translation of this manual is on p. 63.

[44] John Harvey Gray and Lourdes Gray with Steven McFadden and Elisabeth Clark, *Hand to Hand, The Longest-Practicing Reiki Master Tells His Story* (Gray, 2002), p. 93.

[45] Rand, "Origin of the Usui Reiki Master Symbol," p. 34-35.

[46] Before she died, Takata Sensei created a list of the twenty-two Masters she had initiated. They are: George Araki (deceased), Dorothy Baba (deceased), Ursula Baylow (deceased), Rick Bockner, Barbara Brown (deceased), Fran Brown (deceased), Patricia Ewing, Phyllis Lei Furumoto, Beth Gray (deceased), John Gray (deceased), Iris Ishikura (deceased), Harry Kuboi, Ethel Lombardi (deceased), Barbara McCullough (deceased), Mary McFadyen, Paul Mitchell, Bethel Phaigh (deceased), Barbara Weber Ray, Shinobu Saito, Kay Yamashita (Mrs. Takata's sister), Virginia Samdahl (deceased), and Wanja Twan.

information that has taken a long time to reach the West. In addition to the reasons for this mentioned earlier, there are a number of others. After Hayashi Sensei died and World War II ended, Takata Sensei stated that all the other Reiki Masters in Japan had died during the war and that she was the only Reiki Master in the world.[47] Therefore, most people refrained from researching the history of Reiki, thinking she was the only authority. Many of the Masters she initiated also discouraged people from doing such research, stating that it was not needed, as their knowledge of Reiki was complete. Add to all this the fact that the Gakkai had become a secret society along with the linguistic, cultural, and geographic barriers that separated the United States from Japan, and it is easy to see why most authors simply accepted her story as true without seeking verification. Most did not realize that the organization started by Usui Sensei still existed in Japan and that contact with them, while difficult, was still possible.

Reiki since Mrs. Takata

Reiki energy is very flexible and creative, treating each unique situation with a unique response and working freely with all other forms of healing. The Reiki energy itself provides a wonderful model for the practice of Reiki. This began to be acknowledged gradually after Takata Sensei passed on. In the mid-1980s, Iris Ishikura, one of Takata's Masters, trained two Reiki Masters at a more reasonable fee and made them promise they would also charge a reasonable fee. The Masters trained by Ishikura at this lower fee began training many other

Masters in turn. Out of this group, many were open to change and began allowing the wisdom of the Reiki energy to guide them in the way they should practice and teach Reiki. Because of this, restrictive rules began to fall away. Reiki classes became more open and more supportive of the learning process. Workbooks were created, notes and tape recordings were allowed, reasonable fees were charged, and many began studying with more than one teacher. All this generated greater respect for Reiki. It also increased people's understanding of Reiki and improved their healing skills. With lower fees, the practice of Reiki began to grow quickly and spread all over the world. It is estimated that there are at least 1,000,000 Reiki Masters in the world today with well over 4,000,000 practitioners, and the numbers continue to grow!

I learned Reiki I on the Big Island of Hawaii in 1981 from Bethel Phaigh, who had learned from Mrs. Takata. In 1982, I received Reiki II from Bethel. I loved Reiki and started a Reiki practice. Because of the high fee for Reiki Master training at that time and other restrictive rules, I did not think that becoming a Reiki Master was part of my spiritual path. However, Reiki has a way of guiding us in the way we should go, and through a number of coincidences and fortunate circumstances I met Diane McCumber in 1989. She was a Reiki Master of the Ishikura lineage and was charging a very reasonable fee to train Reiki Masters. I took her training and began to teach.

I chose to allow the Reiki energy to guide how I would teach. Rather than adhere strictly to the rules set by Takata Sensei, I wanted to do everything I could to help my students learn Reiki and use it in a way that

---

[47] Graham, "Mrs. Takata Opens Minds to Reiki." This is also stated on her Reiki flyers dated July 1975 and June 1976.

was right for them. If they wanted to start a Reiki practice or to teach, then I wanted them to be as successful as possible.

To further this purpose, I took everything I had learned about Reiki to that point, organized the information and placed it in a class workbook that included drawings of the Reiki hand positions, which I then gave to my Reiki students. I have continued to expand and update the workbook until it evolved into the workbook you are reading now.

From the beginning, I encouraged students to take notes and to tape record my classes; I openly answered all questions and actively encouraged my students to do well. I taught the value of developing one's intuition and having confidence in one's experience and personal decision-making abilities. Knowing that one can always learn more, I continued to study Reiki from others and eventually took the Master Training from four additional Masters including two from Japan. This added to my understanding of Reiki, as each teacher had gained many unique insights about how Reiki works and how to practice it. I make it a point to acknowledge the value of other teachers and practitioners. In my travels, I continue to exchange Reiki information with them, looking for new information to use and pass on to others.

Because I based my Reiki practice on the process of working in harmony with the qualities and values apparent in Reiki energy and following Reiki's guidance in carrying out my plans, my classes were filled with students right from the beginning.

A newsletter was started in 1990 that continued to grow in size and readership and in 2002 became the *Reiki News Magazine*.

Wanting to maintain high standards for Reiki, I started a teacher certification program (now called our Professional Licensed Teachers program) that required additional training and takes about three years to complete.

In 1995 a website was started (www. reiki.org) that now offers over 300 free articles on Reiki and lots of resources for those wanting to practice or teach Reiki. We also have a web store, which offers class workbooks, Reiki tables, and other products. (www.reikiwebstore.com)

We began the Center for Reiki Research in 2009 (www.centerforreikiresearch.org). Staffed by seven Ph.D qualified researchers, it contains references and summaries of all Reiki research studies published in peer-reviewed journals, a description of over 70 hospital Reiki programs, and many useful articles and other features to help those interested in promoting an evidence-based understanding of Reiki. We've also started our own research study on pain in orthopedic patients due to be completed in 2012.

In 2010, we created a professional Reiki Membership Association (www. reikimembership.com). The current membership of over 1800 Reiki practitioners and teachers offers Reiki sessions and classes across the U.S. and in some foreign countries.

Pictures from Mt. Kurama

Mt. Kurama

Entrance to Kurama Temple

Shrine at San-mon Station honoring Sonten. The deity is Vaisravana. The three symbols on the disks represent power on the left, light in the middle behind the deity and love on the right. The love symbol looks very similar to the mental/emotional symbol of Reiki II.

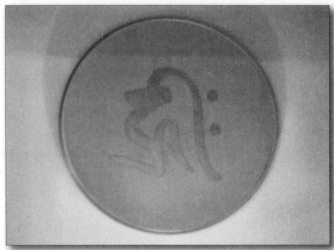

A closer look at the love symbol hrih located in the Tendai temple

One of three giant cedar trees part way up the mountain

Meditation Waterfall

Main Hall

View from Main Hall

Spiral Tiger in front
of Main Hall

Ritual Bell

Roots on the path near
the top of the mountain

Okunoin Mao-den Shrine
at the top of Mt. Kurama

Looking out from
Okunoin Mao-den

Saihoji Temple in
Tokyo where the
Usui Memorial is located

Notes

32

Chapter 3
The International Center for Reiki Training

In 1988 I founded the Center for Spiritual Development. In 1991 the name was changed to the Center for Reiki Training as Reiki became our only focus. In 1997, because of classes that were being taught abroad, "International" was added to our name.

The Reiki training offered by the International Center for Reiki Training is based on the Usui/Holy Fire system of Reiki. However, the Center has also added innovations that have been proven to increase Reiki's effectiveness as a healing art. These include many of the Japanese Reiki Techniques including Byosen Scanning, Reiji-ho, Gyoshi-ho, Kenyoku and Gassho Meditation. Additional training techniques and information included are Aura Clearing that removes negative psychic energy, Healing Attunements, and acknowledgment of the role played by spiritual beings in the healing process.

The attunement process used by the Center in all Reiki Level I, II, ART, and Master classes is a combination of the Western style of the Usui system and the Holy Fire system. In the Reiki Master class, the Usui/Holy Fire method of giving attunements is taught along with the Western system of attunements as taught by Takata Sensei. Students wishing to practice the Takata system of Reiki can easily do so as all additions to the Takata system are clearly explained in class.

Additions the Center has made to the Usui/Holy Fire system have come from inner guidance and a desire to provide greater value. They were added only after they had been thoroughly tested and were proven to enhance healing. The following techniques are ones developed at the Center.

Scanning

Scanning is a way of finding those places in yourself or others that are most in need of healing, then administering Reiki to them. Chapter 6 explains Scanning in detail. (We now use the Byosen method of Scanning.)

Aura Clearing

The presence of negative psychic energy in the body or the aura is the cause of most illness and dysfunction. We therefore developed Aura Clearing, a Reiki technique for removing negative psychic energy. Formerly called Reiki psychic surgery, this highly effective process uses Reiki energy to empower the hands so that practitioners can grasp negative psychic energy within or around themselves or others and send it up to the light. The positive results of this process in healing and well-being are immediately apparent. Reiki Aura Clearing is taught in Advanced Reiki Training. (see Appendix C)

Healing Attunement

A special healing attunement process has also been developed. The Healing Attunement uses the same high-frequency energies used in the initiations, but only for healing. This process opens a spiritual door through which powerful, higher frequency Reiki energies are able to flow. These higher frequencies allow the Reiki guides to work more effectively. Because the healing attunements do not initiate a person into Reiki, they can be given to anyone and are especially useful prior to a regular Reiki session. The Healing Attunement process is taught in the Reiki III/Master class. (see Appendix C)

Three-Step Session

A three-step session is recommended for those who have taken ART/Master training. The Healing Attunement is given first, followed by Aura Clearing and then a regular Reiki session using all the hand positions. This is a powerful combination that speeds up the healing process so that fewer sessions are needed and deeper healing takes place.

Becoming a Reiki Master/Teacher

The Center actively encourages and supports students to become Reiki Masters and teachers if they feel guided to do so. After taking Reiki I & II and taking time to practice and gain experience, individuals can go on to take ART/Master training. They can then begin teaching on their own as independent Reiki Masters, with the option of joining the Reiki Membership Association (www.reikimembership.com).

Many who take the Master training do not intend to teach but do so so they can to use the increased healing energies, symbols and skills for their own healing, to help friends and family, and to improve their healing practice.

Holy Fire Karuna Reiki®

Holy Fire Karuna Reiki® training is an advanced training course offered only to Reiki Masters. It strengthens one's healing energy, allowing it to work more deeply and produce beneficial results more quickly. Eight healing symbols and one master symbol are taught in two levels. Each symbol has a distinctive purpose and vibration. These additional healing tools help one be a more effective healer. Karuna Reiki® is the next step beyond the Reiki Master level. (see Appendix C for more details).

Holy Fire Reiki

The Holy Fire system of Reiki was added to our Reiki classes in January, 2014. It consists of a new symbol that represents a more refined energy that comes from a higher level of consciousness. It brings about more refined levels of healing in the client, works continuously within those who have it and has many other wonderful attributes. It is used in the attunements given in Reiki I&II and ART and is received in the Master levels through an ignition process. Read www.reiki.org/holyfire.html for more information.

Reiki Membership Association

The purpose of the Reiki Membership Association (RMA), begun in 2010, is to promote the professional practice of Reiki. It includes membership requirements, a code of ethics, and standards of practice. A key feature of the RMA is the membership list, which is viewed by over 400 people a day who are in search of qualified Reiki practitioners and teachers. Being listed on our membership list provides an effective way to advertise your Reiki business. Also included is a membership certificate, a professionally created brochure to promote your practice, and a logo to place on your website, business cards, or letterhead paper. The cost of membership is very reasonable. (see www.reikimembership.com to join)

The Center Licensed Teachers Program

The Center Licensed Teachers program is an advanced curriculum of study that takes at least three years to complete. Students must take all our classes—Reiki I & II, Advanced Reiki Training, Reiki Master, and Karuna Reiki® Master—review each class, take a written examination, write a paper, and document a minimum of 100 complete Reiki sessions. They then co-teach each class before teaching it on their own.

To maintain their license, teachers must review classes once a year and turn in class reviews from each student taught. They agree to support the Center Philosophy and Purpose, the Original Reiki Ideals, and to work on their own personal healing. They also agree to abide by a code of ethics and to teach the required subjects for each class. As long as those subjects are covered in class, teachers are free to add meditations or other healing techniques they have found to be useful.

All Reiki Groups Have Value

We affirm that all Reiki practitioners and teachers are being guided by Reiki energy to practice and teach Reiki in a way that is exactly right for them. We also affirm that all Reiki practitioners and groups are working to heal themselves, each other, and the planet. Because of this, we honor and respect all Reiki practitioners, teachers and groups regardless of lineage or organizational affiliation. We have focused on making our system of Reiki the best we can, based on our inner guidance and our experience. We also affirm that Reiki students are capable of deciding for themselves which system or teacher is right for them. We encourage all Reiki students to study with more than one teacher or system if they are guided to do so.

Love grants in a moment what toil can hardly achieve in an age.

—JOHANN WOLFGANG VON GOETHE

The Center Philosophy

- Honesty and clarity in one's thinking.
- Willingness to recognize prejudice in oneself and replace it with truth and love.
- Compassion for those who have decided not to do this.
- Speaking the truth without judgment or blame.
- Respecting others' right to form their own values and beliefs.
- Placing greater value on learning from experience and inner guidance than on the teachings of an outside authority.
- Basing the value of a theory or technique on the verifiable results it helps one achieve.
- Being open to results rather than attached to them.
- Taking personal responsibility for one's situation in life.
- Assuming that one has the resources to resolve any problem encountered, or the ability to develop those resources.
- Using negative and positive experiences to heal and to grow.
- Trusting completely in the Higher Power regardless of the name one uses.
- Complete expression of Love as the highest goal.

The Center Purpose

- To establish and maintain standards for teaching Reiki.
- To train and license Reiki teachers.
- To create instructional manuals for use in Reiki classes.
- To encourage the establishment of Reiki support groups where people can give and receive Reiki sessions.
- To help people develop and use their Reiki skills.
- To encourage students to become successful Reiki teachers if they are guided to do so.
- To research new information about Reiki and to develop new techniques to improve its use.
- To openly acknowledge the value provided by all Reiki people regardless of their lineage or affiliation.
- To promote friendly cooperation among all Reiki practitioners and teachers toward the goal of healing ourselves and Planet Earth through the use of Reiki.

Notes

Notes

Part II

Elements of a Reiki Session

Chapter 4
Using Reiki

Reiki is an easy healing technique to use. After receiving the Reiki attunement, all that is necessary to start Reiki flowing is to request it to do so. Just ask or intend that it begin to flow and it will. This can be done simply by saying the word "Reiki" to yourself at the beginning of a healing session. Reiki is always ready to flow, and it will do so whenever you want it to. Simply placing your hands on someone with the intention of giving a session will be enough to start it flowing. It is not necessary to meditate or concentrate or go into an altered state to use Reiki. Reiki flows so easily that just thinking or talking about it turns it on. In fact, as I write this section of the manual I feel Reiki flowing through me simply because I am thinking about it.

One thing that sometimes happens, especially in groups, is that the people giving Reiki will start talking. This tends to focus attention away from the client and can also decrease the value of the session. Although Reiki will flow when you are talking, it works much better when you are in a meditative state, allowing your consciousness to merge with the Reiki energy.

When giving a Reiki session, it is important to keep your fingers together. This will concentrate the energy and create a stronger flow. Be aware of the sensations in your hands such as warmth, tingling, vibrations, pulsations, or a flow of energy.

You may also feel Reiki flowing through other parts of your body. As you dwell on Reiki, your mind will begin to be aware of the Reiki consciousness. You may experience this as feelings of relaxation, joy, love, well-being, security, unlimited potential, freedom, creativity, beauty, balance, harmony, and other positive states. Allow these feelings to become your feelings. If other thoughts come up, gently brush them away and bring your attention back to the consciousness of Reiki. As you do this, not only will you be allowing Reiki to flow more strongly, you will also be receiving a deep healing.

By meditating on the consciousness of Reiki, you will also be entering a state of mind that will allow your Reiki guides to work more closely with you. They will be better able to channel the Reiki through you as well as send it directly to the client.

The most important way to increase the effectiveness of Reiki is to invite it to come from a place of love, compassion, and kindness within you. This will create a feeling of emotional safety for clients, encouraging them to more fully accept the Reiki energy. It will also open the doors to your healing potential, increasing and providing a deeper healing for you!

Another interesting effect is that Reiki sometimes flows out the bottom of your feet. If you feel this happening, feel free to use your feet to give Reiki, too. By standing close to the client, the Reiki that flows from your feet will treat the client's aura before entering the body where it is needed, or it may simply travel up the outside of your legs and be added to the Reiki coming from your hands.

The question sometimes comes up as to the minimum and maximum amount of time that Reiki should be given. Since Reiki is guided by spiritual consciousness, it can never cause harm. You can never give too little or too much Reiki. If all you have is a few minutes to give Reiki, go ahead. Reiki will always help. You never can tell how much good even a short session will provide. While specific results cannot be guaranteed, short sessions of a few minutes or less have relieved headaches and toothaches, healed bee stings, stopped bleeding, and even set and mended broken bones along with many other valuable results. On the other hand, sessions of several hours or longer can only improve the value of Reiki. You will not overcharge the client with energy or cause any harm whatsoever by giving long sessions.

Reiki will sometimes flow from your hands to other areas of the body. You and/or your client may sense this happening and it may feel like a warm, relaxing sensation in another area other than where your hands are placed. For example, when the hands are placed on the head, Reiki will treat the head but may also travel to the stomach. Conversely, when the hands are placed on the stomach, Reiki will treat this area but could also travel to the neck. Treating the feet can also result in Reiki flowing to the back, etc.

This doesn't always happen, but when it does, it is because you have placed your hands on an energetic doorway that links the two areas of the body or energy field together. The energetic doorway opens to a bridge or pathway through which Reiki flows to the other area that is in need of Reiki. The body and energy fields are holistic in nature and interconnect within themselves in ways that don't always seem to make sense, but finding where the doorway is located for a specific condition allows us to provide a more effective Reiki session. These energetic doorways are specific to the individual client and could change as the client heals. It is important to understand that this doesn't mean that Reiki will always flow to wherever it is needed as some have thought. It simply means that the best place to treat an area isn't always over the area where the symptoms exist. Because of this, the best way to treat a condition is to use one's intuition to find the energetic doorway to

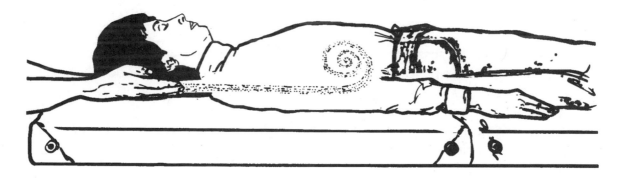

Reiki sometimes flows to other areas in addition to where the hands are placed

the cause of the condition, which may be in another location on the body or aura, and place your hands there.

Your intuition can play an important role when treating specific symptoms. This method was taught to me by my first Reiki teacher, Bethel Phaigh who was taught by Takata Sensei. First try placing your hands over the area of concern. If you feel a lot of Reiki flowing, then stay there. However, if Reiki does not flow well, ask the client what he or she is feeling. If neither of you feels that Reiki is treating the area of concern, ask your intuition to show you the best place to treat the condition and move your hands wherever you are directed. If you feel more Reiki flowing there and the client reports the symptoms subsiding, then you will know your intuition is working well.

Sometimes, the best place to treat a condition is not where the symptoms are manifesting. Always remember to ask to be guided to the best place to treat the condition. You can use the Byosen scanning technique or Reiji ho explained in Chapter 6, or simply ask to be guided to the right place. Trust in your inner guidance even if you think it is illogical or wrong or just the product of your imagination. As you gain experience using this technique, you'll become confident in the use of your intuition.

Another way to treat the energetic doorways is to give a full body session using all the hand positions. By doing this, some of the hand positions you use will be right over an energetic doorway, and when this happens, you will most likely feel the stronger flow and will know to stay there longer.

The hand positions for treating oneself and others are in Chapters 6–8. Keep in mind that they are meant as a general guide only. You do not need to strictly adhere to them. Use your intuition. If you feel guided to leave out a position or to add a new one, go ahead. A good guideline is to stay in each position a minimum of three minutes to allow time for Reiki to start flowing. If it flows strongly, then most likely you have found an energetic doorway and in the context of a standard, ninety-minute session, stay a maximum of ten minutes at this position and move on. If you were to stay longer, you might not have time to give a complete session unless you intended to go longer than 90 minutes. At the end of the session, if you have extra time return to the areas where Reiki flowed strongly to give those areas additional Reiki. Then make a note in your client documentation form about where Reiki flowed strongest so you can check these areas during future sessions.

There is a light in this world . . . a healing spirit much stronger than any darkness we may encounter. We sometimes lose sight of this force . . . where there is suffering, too much pain. And suddenly the spirit will emerge . . . through lives of ordinary people, and answer in extraordinary ways. God speaks in the silence of the heart and we listen.

—MOTHER TERESA

Notes

Chapter 5
The Reiki Symbols

There are no symbols in First Degree Reiki, and they are not necessary to give a Reiki treatment. However, the symbols that are given in Second Degree Reiki and beyond, and the attunements that empower them, add to the strength and value of the system of Reiki healing.

Reiki symbols are sacred. It is part of the Reiki tradition that they be kept confidential. They are only revealed to those who have taken Second Degree Reiki or higher and received the attunement that empowers them. The reason for the secrecy is two-fold. First there is a personal issue. By keeping the symbols secret, you demonstrate your respect for them. If others reveal the symbols or display them in print or on the Internet, this cannot affect your own personal relationship with the symbols. As long as you keep them secret, you are demonstrating your respect.

The second reason for keeping the symbols secret is consideration for others. Since the power of the symbols comes from the attunement, showing them to those who have not received the attunement will not help them and could cause confusion by leading them to believe they already have the entire system and don't need to take the class or receive the attunement. If this happens, then they would miss the real value of Reiki. However, since the symbols aren't shown in this manual, their nature and purpose can be discussed without violating this trust.

It is important to note that the attunement actually empowers the symbols so that they will fulfill their intended purpose; without the attunement, the symbols do not seem to do much. This has been verified many times. Students have been given the symbols to memorize before the attunement process takes place. Many have been psychic and some have been healers who are able to see and feel the Reiki energies. All report similar effects. Before the attunement, the symbols don't seem to have much an influence on the Reiki energies. After the attunement, the effect is definitely there.

Reiki symbols are transcendental. Rather than affecting only the subconscious mind as most symbols do, the Reiki symbols connect directly to Spiritual Consciousness and affect the source of Reiki, changing the effect of the Reiki energies. Whenever a Reiki symbol is used by someone who has Second Degree Reiki or higher, the Rei or Spiritual Consciousness responds by changing the way the Reiki energy functions. This process operates under a divine covenant or sacred agreement between the Source of Reiki and those who have Second Degree Reiki or higher. A person does not have to be in an altered state for the symbols to work. They work automatically, every time they are used.

Reiki symbols are like keys that open doors to higher levels of healing. They can also be thought of as buttons: whenever you "push" one, you automatically get the energy of that symbol.

Of course, the symbols must be used correctly to activate them. But activating them is really very simple. In fact they are activated simply by your intention to use them. And because it is your intention that activates the symbols, there is no exact and perfect way you must draw them in order for them to work. In other words, you do not have to draw each line to exactly the correct length or at the exact angle. As long as the symbol can be identified as the one you are using, it will work. Even Takata Sensei didn't draw the symbols the same way each time and because of this there are also some differences between the symbols of the original twenty-two Masters she taught.

However, if you have respect for Reiki and if you want to use the symbols properly, it's important that you learn how to draw the symbols correctly so that all the lines are present and drawn in the right sequence. The reason they need to be drawn in the correct sequence is because writing kanji characters or drawing out the symbols is considered to be an art form and having a smooth rhythmic flow to your pen or brush or hand is important in maintaining the right energy for each character or symbol.

When a Reiki Master shows the Reiki symbols to a student and gives the attunement for them, an imprinting takes place that links the image the student has been shown to the metaphysical energies the symbol represents. This makes use of the stimulus/response mechanism in the brain. Whenever a specific stimulus repeatedly accompanies a particular experience, a relationship develops between the stimulus and a person's response to it. Pavlov demonstrated this in his famous experiment. Whenever he fed his dog, he rang a bell. After doing this over and over, all he had to do was ring the bell and the dog salivated. Because the energies of the Reiki attunement are of a transcendental nature, this process is speeded up so that a person needs to be exposed to the symbols only briefly. Then, during the attunement, the energy the symbol represents comes down and links itself to the symbol located in the brain. Then after this, whenever the student thinks of the symbol, the energy the symbol represents automatically begins to flow.

Because Takata Sensei did not allow her students to make copies of the symbols, they had to memorize them. Many did not have perfect memories and when the symbols were passed on from teacher to student over and over again, with no one being allowed to write them down, many variations developed. We now find that the symbols used by some Reiki teachers look nothing like the original symbols used by Usui Sensei, yet they work just the same. However, if one calls what one is practicing and teaching Usui Reiki, then out of respect for Usui Sensei and out of respect for ones students, it is important that the symbols one uses at least look similar to those used by Usui Sensei.

We have received many requests to be shown how the symbols were originally drawn. Because of this, we've made a copy of the Reiki symbols as drawn by Takata Sensei available for download on our website in the free download section at www.reiki.org. A password is required known only by those who have taken the class so that the privacy requirement is fulfilled.

The following descriptions explain a number of proven uses for the symbols. However, Reiki symbols have their own energy and consciousness, and it is possible to meditate on them and be shown how to use them directly from the Spiritual Consciousness that is inherent in the symbols themselves. Practice the following, but also feel free to experiment with the symbols, and you will discover many more uses.

Activating Reiki Symbols

There are many ways to activate Reiki symbols. You can draw them in the air in front of you or on or near the client. You can also draw them on the palms of your hands before placing your hands on the client. The symbols are best drawn using your whole hand with all the fingers extended. Another way to draw them is using the whole hand but intending that they are being drawn from the palm chakra. You can also activate a symbol by thinking of its name, or by saying it out loud if no one is around or if you are only with persons who have had Reiki II or higher. You can also visualize the symbol or imagine yourself drawing it. Any of these ways will activate Reiki symbols. The important thing is your intention: intend to activate the symbol and it will activate. The above methods are simply ways of expressing your intention.

The Power Symbol

The Power symbol comes from Shintoism, and the Japanese name means "by imperial decree." In Japan, the emperor was considered to be Divine so it can also mean "by decree of the Divine." It was used in a similar way as Christians use Amen or Pagans say So Be It. It was

used at the end of a meeting to empower the plans that were made or to empower a decision.

In Reiki practice, the power symbol is used to increase the power of Reiki or to focus Reiki on a specific location. Anytime you want to increase the strength of the Reiki energy you are giving, just think of the name or visualize the symbol and your Reiki will get stronger! It can also be used to seal the space around the client and prevent the healing energies from leaking away. This can be seen psychically and appears at times as a box of white light or at other times as a sphere of golden light surrounding the client. The power symbol can be used anytime during a session but is especially effective if used at the beginning to increase the power and at the end to seal in the healing energies. The power symbol can be used to clear a room of negative psychic energy and seal it in light, making it a sacred space. It can be used to protect yourself, your loved ones, your car, your home, or anything you value. Because Reiki works on all levels, the protection it provides is also on all levels and includes protection from physical harm, as well as protection from verbal and emotional confrontations and from psychic attack. You can also use the power symbol to bless others—just think of its name as you shake hands or hug someone you want to bless. Experiment and you will find many other uses.

The Mental/Emotional Symbol

During my first trip to Japan, I discovered a symbol that looked very similar to the Mental/Emotional symbol. It was in a Tendai Buddhist temple on Mt. Kurama. The symbol is a Sanskrit seed syllable called hrih, which means love and harmony, and is the likely origin of the Mental/Emotional symbol (See page 28 and 126). The Japanese name of this symbol means "bad habit." This symbol is used in emotional and mental healing to heal bad habits but also has many other uses. It balances the right and left sides of the brain, bringing harmony and peace. It is especially useful for healing relationship problems. It can be used with any sort of mental/emotional distress such as nervousness, fear, depression, anger, sadness, and others. Psychically, the energy of this symbol sometimes takes the form of a bubble coming out of the heart chakra of the practitioner for emotional healing or out of the solar plexus chakra for mental healing. Sometimes these two energies work together and mix in front of the practitioner before surrounding and/or entering the client. This symbol can be used to heal addictions as well as problems with weight loss or smoking. It can be used to improve memory and is especially useful at those odd moments when one loses the car keys or forgets a person's name. It can be used to enhance the use of affirmations, causing them to enter more deeply into the subconscious mind. It is also wonderful for studying, learning, or taking tests.

Healing Unwanted Habits Including Weight Loss, Cigarettes, Alcohol, and Drugs

The mental/emotional symbol can be used to change or eliminate unwanted habits. Write your name on a piece of paper or a note card along with a description of the unwanted habit and then draw the mental/emotional healing symbol in the air over the paper. Then hold the paper between your hands,

treating it with Reiki. This will send Reiki to the parts of your mind and emotions that relate to the unwanted habit, and will begin healing them. Do this for twenty minutes or longer each day. Carry the paper with you. If you feel the unwanted compulsion come up during the day, take out the paper and Reiki it again.

Example: If you want to lose weight, write your name on a piece of paper or on a note card. Also write the words "healthy weight loss" then draw the mental/emotional healing symbol in the air above the paper or card. Then give it Reiki by holding it between your hands. Carry the paper with you and do this at least once each day or any time you have a spare moment and also before each meal. If you are tempted to eat something not on your diet, before you do so, take out your paper or card and give it Reiki. After doing this, you'll find it much easier to stay on your diet, to eat less, and to eat only healthy foods.

Using the mental/emotional symbol to eliminate unwanted habits is an important activity and is well worth the time it takes to do it. I suggest choosing one unwanted habit to work on at a time and continue until you have transformed it into a healthy habit. Then go on to another unwanted habit. As you do this, you will build momentum and your enthusiasm for the process will grow, making it easier to continue. Over time, your life will be transformed!

The Distant Healing Symbol

The Distant symbol is derived from a Japanese spiritual saying and is composed of Japanese kanji characters. The name is written in romanji, which is the phonetic use of the Western alphabet to write out kanji characters. The Japanese name of this symbol means "The origin of all is pure consciousness." Pure consciousness exists at the deepest level of being and at this level there is no time or space. This symbol is used to send Reiki to others at a distance. You can send Reiki to people who are across the room, across town, or even in other parts of the country or the world. Distance is no barrier when using this symbol. Sometimes a picture of the client is used in conjunction with the symbol.

I have often used the distant healing symbol with my clients who are coming for a Reiki session. By sending Reiki to them while they are on their way to the appointment, I find they always arrive calm and relaxed. I have also used Reiki for past-life regression, hypnosis, and guided meditation. By using the distant healing symbol with the mental/emotional healing symbol, I am able to send Reiki to them during the session from across the room to help facilitate the healing process.

This sometimes has interesting effects. Without my telling them what I am doing, the Reiki energy will often blend with the person's inner imagery and actually become part of the scenario they are experiencing. Having its own wisdom, the Reiki energy knows exactly how to do this. Sometimes they see it surrounding them in the form of a protective white mist. It has also worked to empower them by flowing through them and out of their hands, which they then visually direct spontaneously toward the area of difficulty in their inner experience to help solve the problem.

The distant symbol can also be used to bridge time. You can use it to send Reiki into the future. If you know you will be involved in an important activity in the future, and you know the date and time of the event, you can send Reiki to the event so that it will be there to help you when the time comes. When it is used in this way, it is as though the Reiki energy is stored up in a battery. When the time comes, its healing energy descends to surround you and help you. People have used this technique to help with job interviews, tests, trips to the dentist, surgery, or other important events.

This symbol can also be used to send Reiki into the past. If you had a traumatic experience in the past and you know the approximate date, you can use the distant symbol to send Reiki back to heal the trauma. It often helps if you have a picture of yourself close to the time the trauma occurred. If you don't know the date and don't have a picture, it will still work simply by naming the problem and asking that Reiki go to the cause and heal it. This technique can also be used to heal problems that stem from past lives.

Use of the mental/emotional symbol with the distant symbol can improve the healing process when working with emotional issues at a distance or in the past or future.

The distant symbol can also be used like a homing device. If you don't know the area of the body to treat for a particular condition, or where the cause of a problem is, just use the distant symbol, asking it to send the Reiki energy to the cause of the problem, and Reiki will go there without you needing to know where or what the cause is.

The distant symbol can also be used for exorcism and spirit release work. This is a simple process that is very powerful. It is not based on a contest between you and the spirit—therefore it does not drain your energy or place you in harm's way. Just use the distant symbol to send Reiki to the spirit, then call on an Illumined Being or Ascended Master and ask him or her to take the spirit up into the light. Continue sending Reiki for several more minutes or until you feel the process is complete. The Illumined Being or Ascended Master will do all the work and deal with the spirit in exactly the right way to create a healing for both the person and the spirit.

Using the Distant Healing Symbol

Sending distant Reiki is a two-step process. First, establish the connection by using the distant symbol with the person's name or picture. Then send Reiki. Reiki will begin going to the person and continue as long as you intend to send Reiki. Here are several ways to send distant Reiki:

- Use a picture of the person. Place the picture in front of you and draw the distant symbol in the air, imagining you are drawing it over the picture. Then beam Reiki with your hands toward the picture and it will go to that person.

- Do the above, only hold the picture between your hands and request Reiki to flow to the person.

- Write the person's name on a piece of paper, draw the distant healing symbol, and hold the paper between your hands.

- Simply hold your hands up in the direction in which you imagine the person to be, draw the distant healing symbol, and beam Reiki to him or her.

- Use a teddy bear as a stand-in or surrogate for the person. Say the person's name three times, then draw the distant healing symbol down the front of the teddy bear's body. Then do a standard treatment using all the hand positions on the teddy bear intending the treatment to go to the person. It is also possible to do Byosen Scanning with the teddy bear. If you do not have a teddy bear, you may use a pillow instead.

- While driving, intend that the steering wheel represents the person you want to send Reiki to. Think of the distant symbol or say its name, then say the name of the person you want to send Reiki to. Reiki will flow to the person while you are driving and have both hands on the wheel!

- Experiment sending Reiki to Jesus, Buddha, God, the full moon, the earth, pagan gods, your spirit guides, angels, and others. People who have done this type of distant healing report receiving tremendous healing back from these high, spiritual beings. Doing this also creates a strong connection so that your prayers to them are empowered.

- Use the distant healing symbol to send Reiki to people you knew in the past or to people on TV or in the newspapers, especially those who are injured or otherwise in need of help.

- Send Reiki to national or world crisis situations using one of the above techniques.

While it is best to send distant Reiki only to those who have requested it as they will be the most receptive, there may be times when you will want to help someone who is not aware that you could help her or for whom requesting help may be difficult. People in comas can't request help, but still might want it if they knew about the possibility. Also, you may want to send Reiki to heal the earth or to a crisis situation. In these cases, just say a prayer asking for permission to send Reiki. You may get permission or you may not, but it is important to follow your inner guidance. Remember, Reiki can do no harm. Also, Reiki respects a person's free will. If you send Reiki to someone who does not want it, the Reiki will not affect them.

Group Distant Healing

Distant healing can be sent by a group of Reiki II practitioners with powerful results. Just sit in a circle and place the name or picture of the person you want to send Reiki to in the middle. This technique will also work to send Reiki to many people at the same time. Have everyone draw the distant symbol and say its name three times, then beam Reiki to the picture(s) or name(s) in the center. Remember, Reiki works by intention. Just use your imagination to think of other ways to send distant Reiki.

Empowering Goals

If you have been blocked in the achievement of a particular goal, it usually means there is something that needs to heal before you will be able to achieve that goal. In addition, the achievement of any goal will be easier

if all its aspects are surrounded with the loving, harmony-producing energy of Reiki.

Write your name on a piece of paper or a note card. Also write down a name for your goal, or just a description of it. If dates are involved, write them down too. Then draw all three symbols in the air above the paper or card and Reiki it for twenty minutes or more each day. Carry the card or paper with you wherever you go. Give it Reiki whenever you have a spare moment. Continue to actively work to achieve your goal.

As you do this, you'll find everything working much better. You'll be more alert to the resources around you that can help achieve your goal and you'll tend to find yourself in the right place at the right time to take advantage of events favorable to your purpose. If the goal is in harmony with your higher good, you will achieve it!

Reiki is a powerful healing energy that has many possibilities for the innovative practitioner. It is exciting that something as valuable as Reiki is now widely available.

If we are to solve the personal and global problems that face us, it is important to make effective use of the healing resources available to us and to be thankful for the techniques that are now surfacing from ancient knowledge. These are the most interesting of times, filled with the possibility of important discoveries, the development of higher consciousness, and the transformation of society. Let us take charge of our lives and create an exciting adventure out of the challenges we face!

Notes

Chapter 6
Japanese Reiki Techniques

The Japanese Reiki Techniques were the central part of Usui Reiki Ryoho as taught by Usui Sensei and Hayashi Sensei. I learned them in 1999 when I invited Arjava Petter and his wife Chetna Kobayashi to come to the U.S. to teach them. They returned in 2000 to teach again, and I had the opportunity to take the class and review it many times. In addition, I've taken Reiki I&II from Chiyoko Yamaguchi and her son Tadao and I've also taken Reiki Master training from Hiroshi Doi, and in both classes, the Japanese Reiki Techniques were taught. I have practiced and taught these techniques and find that they add value to one's Reiki practice.

Usui Sensei had a Reiki handbook he gave to all his students. His Reiki handbook is called *Reiki Ryoho Hikkei* (*Reiki Healing Art Handbook*).[1] In the handbook are exercises and techniques that he included in his Reiki training. In addition, every president of the Usui Reiki Ryoho Gakkai has had a handbook they have given to their Reiki students. The information in this section originally came from these handbooks.

Usui Sensei practiced Reiki in a less structured way than did Takata Sensei. He relied more on his intuition and inner sensitivity when giving sessions. He did not use the standard set of hand positions as taught by Takata Sensei. These hand positions were something she created as a way to simplify how she taught Reiki. However, he did develop

hand positions for specific illnesses and conditions based on his experience. They are similar to those in the *Hayashi Reiki Ryoho Shinshin* (*Hayashi Reiki Healing Guide*), a translation of which is located at the end of this section.

The standard hand placements taught by Takata Sensei have value in that by treating the whole person they automatically treat the areas most in need. They also create balance and increase vitality, and create a reservoir of Reiki energy that continues to heal and energize the person even after the session is over. The hand positions for specific illnesses and conditions in the Hayashi Reiki Healing Guide are also useful when a client comes with a specific condition and one has difficulty discovering the best places to treat using the intuitive methods.

Reiji-ho and Byosen Scanning are useful because they allow a practitioner to go immediately to those areas most in need of healing. These methods can also increase the client's awareness about where they are out of balance.

One way to combine these various methods in a Reiki session is to start with Gassho, followed by Reiji-ho or Byosen Scanning, and ending with the standard hand placements shown in Chapter 9. You can also give an entire session using the Three Pillars of Reiki. Others may find another combination more useful. As you practice all the methods in this manual and become familiar with them, you will be better able to develop your own style based on the techniques that work best for you.

[1] For a translation of two parts of his manual, see *Reiki News Magazine*, Summer 2006, 47.

The following are the Japanese Reiki techniques of Usui Sensei:

The Three Pillars of Reiki

According to Usui Sensei, Gassho, Reiji-ho, and Chiryo constitute The Three Pillars of Reiki. Making use of these techniques gives the practitioner several advantages. They prepare the practitioner to give Reiki, increase the flow of Reiki energy, and determine where the client needs Reiki. Engaging the three pillars helps to ensure that the session is given while one is in a "healing" state.

Gassho meditation

Gassho means "two hands coming together." Usui Sensei called this technique the first pillar of Reiki, and he practiced it twice a day. It is also mentioned on the Usui memorial stone where it states:

"Mornings and evenings, sit in the Gassho position and repeat these words [the Reiki ideals] out loud and in your heart." This is a special meditation to attune one to the spirit of Reiki. It is done as a regular meditation everyday and also is part of other techniques listed below. It clears the mind, opens the heart and other chakras, and

strengthens one's Reiki energy. A wonderful stillness will develop inside along with the awareness of increased inner space.

1. This meditation can be done standing, but most prefer sitting. It is done for 10–20 minutes per session. However if time is a factor, 5 minutes has value.
2. Close your eyes. Fold your hands in the prayer position with your fingers pointing up and your thumbs touching the heart chakra at the middle of your chest.
3. Focus all your attention on the space between the palm chakras. (A variation is to focus on the middle fingers).
4. If thoughts arise, acknowledge them and then gently brush them aside and refocus on the space between the palm chakras.
5. As you continue to practice, you will find that you can hold your attention on the space between the palm chakras for longer and longer periods of time without thoughts arising.
6. It is important to accept that thoughts will arise. When this happens, do not think you have made a mistake, as this is completely normal. However, as soon as you realize that you are focusing on a thought, brush it aside and refocus on the space between the palm chakras.
7. When you have reached the end of the meditation, take a couple of deep breaths, bring your attention to your eyes, and open them slowly.

Reiji-ho

Reiji-ho means *indication of the spirit* and is the second pillar of Reiki. This is a technique that allows you to be intuitively guided to where a person needs Reiki. It can also be used to determine the best area to place the hands to help specific illnesses and conditions. Additionally, it can be used to determine how to carry out a session for a client—which symbols and techniques to use.

1. Do the Gassho meditation, but only for a minute or so.
2. Say a prayer, giving thanks to the source of Reiki and asking it to begin flowing now.
3. Say a prayer on behalf of the client, asking that she or he be completely healed.
4. Move your hands up so the thumbs touch the third eye (the area between the eye brows) as in Fig 2 for Byosen Scanning. Ask Reiki to guide your hands to where they are needed. You could also ask to be shown the best places to treat a specific condition or which symbols and techniques to use in the session.
5. Follow your inner guidance and allow your hands to be directed by Reiki. Notice any internal impressions you may get and use these to improve the session.
6. Use Reiji-ho anytime during the session when you need additional guidance.

Chiryo

This word means "treatment" and is the third pillar of Reiki. The kind of treatment Usui Sensei taught relies on one's inner guidance rather than on a predetermined set of hand positions. In this way, each treatment is unique and focuses on what the client needs to create wholeness. After doing Reiji-ho, continue to follow your inner guidance allowing yourself to

be directed. Treat as many places on the body or in the aura as you feel compelled to. During this process, allow yourself to enter a very relaxed state and to become one with the Reiki energy.

Byosen Scanning

Scanning is a technique I developed at the Center in 1990. When I developed scanning I had been meditating on how Usui Sensei must have practiced Reiki. I was guided to scan the body using the palm of my hand to detect where the person needed Reiki even though this was not part of any of my previous Reiki training. In 1999, we learned from Arjava Petter that Usui Sensei had used a method called Byosen Scanning that was almost exactly the same as the method I had been guided to use.

The word Byosen means "disease line" in Japanese and is a method of using the sensitivity in the hands to discover and treat those areas in need of Reiki.

The attunement allows this process to be more easily accomplished because the attunement not only opens the palm chakras so Reiki can flow; it also heightens their sensitivity to psychic energy.

To scan your client, first place your hands in the Gassho position. (Fig. 1) Say a prayer giving thanks for this opportunity to help another. Ask that the Reiki energy begin to flow in a powerful way. Then bring your hands up so the thumbs touch the third eye area. (Fig. 2) At this point say a prayer, asking to be guided to where the person needs Reiki. Because you are asking to be shown only those places in need of Reiki, you will not be aware of other things—only those areas in need of Reiki. Because of this you will not be distracted by the energy of a chakra or an organ or anything else unless that area needs Reiki. This makes the system more efficient.

Next place your left (or non-dominant) hand about twelve inches away from the top of the person's head. (Fig. 3) Place your consciousness in the palm of your hand and notice how it feels. Then move your hand closer, about three to four inches from the top of the head, and begin moving your hand above the person's face and down toward the feet, continuing to remain about three to four inches away from the body. (Figs. 4–5) Move your hand very slowly and be aware of any changes in energy that register on the palm of your hand. These sensations are called hibiki in Japanese. Where you feel any change at all is a place where the person has a Byosen and needs Reiki. The hibiki may feel like coolness, warmth, tingling, pressure, little electric shocks, pulsations, distortions, irregularities, or a pulling sensation. You may also simply have a knowingness. The change may be very slight, and you may think it is just your imagination or that there is a breeze blowing in the room. However, it is important to ignore these logical distractions and accept what your intuition and heightened sensitivity are telling you.

When you first begin to practice Byosen Scanning, your sensitivity may not be very developed, so you need to pay very close attention. As you practice, your ability to scan the body will improve, and you will gain confidence. After a while, you may even find that you can scan with your eyes and sense where the problems are located, and you could also begin to actually see the negative energy around the distressed areas. Or you may simply know where to treat as soon as you say the prayer. Your ability to do Byosen Scanning will improve as you continue to practice. Over time, some practitioners have become clairvoyant and able to see great detail in the energy patterns around the areas needing healing.

As soon as you find a change in the energy field, move your hand up and down over that area until you find the height at which you feel the most distress. This could be as high as several feet above the body, or you may feel drawn to actually touch the body with your hands. Often the best height is found to be about four inches from the body.

When you find the right height, bring both hands together at this spot and channel Reiki. (Fig. 6) Reiki will heal the aura and chakra(s) and flow into the physical body to work on the organs and tissues and heal them also.

Continue channeling Reiki at the detected spot until you feel the flow of Reiki subsiding or changing. Then re-scan the area to get a better idea of how the healing is progressing. You may find that as you continue, the height needed for healing decreases and the strength of the sensation diminishes. Continue to do Reiki there re-scan periodically until the energy field smooths out, and you no longer feel a hibiki. Afterwards, scan until you find another area in need of healing and do Reiki there. Continue until you have scanned and healed the whole energy field.

There is a more formal method of Byosen Scanning in which the severity of the Byosen can be determined by closely

Byosen Scanning

Figure 1   Figure 2

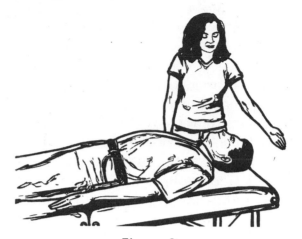

Figure 3

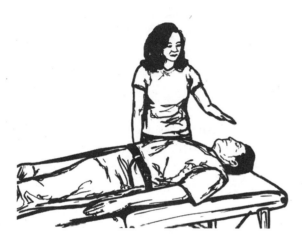

Figure 4

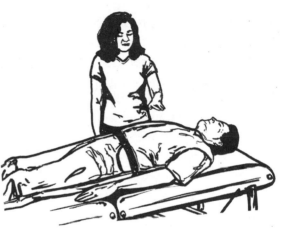

Figure 5

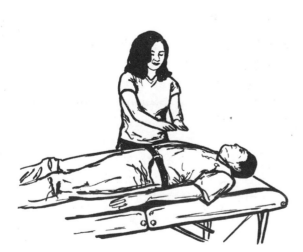

Figure 6

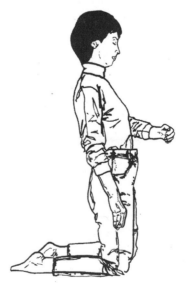

Figure 7

monitoring the hibiki. With this method, there are five levels of hibiki that include heat, strong heat, tingling, pulsation, and discomfort. However, it's possible that with practice, you will develop your own system of monitoring that will give you important information about the Byosen—changes to make in your hand placement, what is happening to it as you give it Reiki, and when the healing is complete. Practice will develop your ability and receiving class instruction can be very helpful in learning this important Reiki technique.

Scanning and healing the energy field is very healthy because the cause of most illnesses and other problems is in the aura. By treating the aura, you will be working on the cause and thereby healing problems before they can manifest in the physical body. Even after a problem has developed in the body, a client will respond better to Reiki if the aura is treated first. By healing the aura first, you will help the person's energy field accept Reiki more completely. The energy will then flow more easily if you choose to do a complete standard treatment as described in Chapter 9. Therefore, if you are going to do both Byosen Scanning and a standard treatment, do the scanning first.

As you interact with the client's energy field, the two of you will become intimately connected. You may become aware of the cause of the distortion and the personal problems connected to it. You may also be given insight into how the problems were created and what the client can do to facilitate the healing. Share this information only if you are guided to do so, and then only with loving kindness, and without judgment. This is sacred work. Always treat the client and the process with great respect.

Self-Scanning

Byosen Scanning can also be done on yourself. Follow the same steps as above including Gassho at the heart and third eye and the prayers, only direct your attention toward yourself. Then administer Reiki when you find the areas in need. (Fig. 7) Self-scanning can bring aspects of yourself into your consciousness that you were not aware of. You will get to know yourself better and be shown new levels of yourself that need healing.

When you find a distortion in your energy field, ask what happened to create it and what you can do to help it heal. Remember: be kind to yourself. Accept whatever is shown to you without judgment or blame. Allow yourself to feel your feelings. Be ready to forgive and to let love in. This can be an intimate process, making you aware of deeper needs, increasing your sensitivity, and facilitating personal growth.

Koki-ho

This is a method that uses the breath and the power symbol or any of the other symbols to heal.

1. Using Byosen Scanning or Reiji-ho, find an area on the client that needs healing. The client may also indicate to you an area in need of healing.
2. Then breathe in using a belly breath and draw the breath all the way down to an area called the Tanden, which is in the belly a little below the navel.
3. Hold your breath a moment and using your tongue and doing the best you can, draw the power symbol or any other symbol you would like to use, on the roof of your mouth.

4. Then vigorously breathe into the area in need of Reiki, contracting the belly as you do so.
5. Imagine you are breathing the symbol into the area.
6. Do this several times if you feel it is necessary.

Kenyoku

This word means "dry bathing" and is a technique for cleansing one's energy before or after a treatment. It can also be used anytime one feels the need to release negative energy.

1. Do a short Gassho meditation.
2. Place your right hand on your left shoulder.

3. Stroke down your chest, across your stomach and end at the right hip.
4. Do the same on the other side.
5. Repeat step #2.
6. Extend your left arm.
7. Place your right hand on your left shoulder.
8. Stroke down your arm all the way to the hand and fingertips. Then fling your right hand out into the air as though you were throwing away any negative energy.
9. Do the same with the right arm.
10. Repeat the stroke down the left arm again.
11. You can also add a short Gassho at the end.

Gyoshi-ho

Gyoshi means to stare and this is a method of sending Reiki with the eyes.

1. Using Byosen Scanning or Reiji-ho or simply by knowing where the client needs healing, decide where you are going to send Reiki.
2. Then focus onto the area in need with your eyes.
3. Allow your eyes to relax and become de-focused.
4. As you do this, meditate on Reiki energy and on your eyes and intend that Reiki flow from your eyes to the area.
5. If any thoughts arise, gently brush them aside in a way that is similar to the process used in Gassho.
6. Do this for several minutes or longer if you are guided to do so.

Gyoshi-ho can be done in a variety of other ways. While giving a hand placement session, in addition to giving Reiki with your hands, stare at the area as you think of your eyes and of Reiki, intending that Reiki flow from your eyes to the area being treated. While giving a Reiki hand session, scan the body with your eyes until you sense another area in need of Reiki. You may see or sense a dark area or simply have knowingness that another area needs Reiki. Stare at the area, thinking of your eyes and intending Reiki to flow from your eyes to the area. If you have seen a dark shape there, you will see it decrease in size or fade away as it is healed. Gyoshi-ho can also be done on yourself.

Jacki-Kiri Joka-ho

Jacki means "negative energy" and Kiri means "to cut." It is a method to release and/or transform negative energy from objects. It can be done with crystals or other objects that you feel need cleansing. This is a very simple and effective method of clearing negative energy from an object.

1. Do a short Gassho meditation, asking the Reiki to be with you.
2. Hold the object in your left or non-dominate hand: In the case of large objects, stand in front of it.
3. Take in a deep belly breath.
4. Then cut through the air about two inches above it three times with a vigorous chopping motion as you continue to hold your breath. Then exhale.
5. In the case of something as large as a house, physically move your hand in the chopping motion, but imagine you are chopping above it.
6. This process can be done at a distance using the distant symbol after the Gassho meditation and imagining you are holding the object or are in its presence. Alternate method: In step 4, cut through the air about two inches above with a vigorous chopping motion, but contract your belly and breathe out. Repeat this three times.

Enkaku chiryo

Enkaku means "sending" and chiryo means "treatment." There are many ways to send distant Reiki. This is the way Usui Sensei practiced it.

1. Get a photo of the person you wish to send distant Reiki to. If you can't get a photo, take a piece of paper and write the person's name on it.
2. Place it in your hand, and in the air above, draw out the distant symbol.
3. Allow Reiki to flow, and it will go directly to the person.

60

4. You can also send distant Reiki by placing the photo or paper in front of you and beaming Reiki to it.

Teddy Bear Technique

You can also give a complete Reiki session to someone at a distance using a teddy bear to represent the person.

1. Place your teddy bear in front of you and prepare to give a distant session by doing a short Gassho meditation.
2. Continue in Gassho position and pray, giving thanks for all the healing your client is about to receive.
3. Then draw the distant symbol down the front of the teddy bear and repeat its name three times.

4. Then make this statement: "As I give a Reiki session to the teddy bear I give a session to (say the persons name)."
5. Add any additional symbols you'd like to use.
6. Proceed to give a complete Reiki session using all the hand positions, and the client will receive it.
7. This method can also be used to do Byosen Scanning at a distance and treat those areas you find that are in need of Reiki.[2]

Japanese Reiki Techniques DVD

A DVD workshop featuring the Japanese Reiki Techniques taught by Arjava Petter and Chetna Kobyashi is available. Please visit www.reikiwebstore.com.

---

[2] Also see page 50.

Pronouncing The Reiki Ideals In Japanese

Below is a guide for pronouncing the Reiki Ideals in Japanese.

"Just for Today" is pronounced: **Kyo dake wa**

"Don't get angry" and is pronounced: **Okolu-na**

"Don't worry" and is pronounced: **Shinpai suna**

"Be grateful" and is pronounced: **Kansha shite**

"Work hard" and is pronounced: **Goo hage me**

"Be kind to others" and is pronounced: **Hito ni shinsetsu ni**

See page vi at the beginning of this manual for the complete text in English and Japanese. To listen to an audio guide to the pronunciation of the ideals, please go to: http://www.reiki.org/JapaneseTechniques/5Principles.html

Hayashi Reiki Healing Guide

This Hayashi Reiki Healing Guide or Hayashi Reiki Ryoho Shinshin[1] as it was originally called in Japan was developed at the Hayashi Reiki Kenkyukai (Institute). At the institute Hayashi Sensei kept detailed records of each patient who came for treatment. This included the illnesses and conditions each had and which hand positions worked the best. It was from this information that the guide was created and he gave a copy to each of his students. However, the guide was meant to be used only if the best places to treat a patient could not be found using byosen scanning or reiji-ho.

Head

1. Head, including brain diseases, headache
   1. Front of jaw
   2. Temples
   3. Back of the Head and back of the neck
   4. Top of the Head

Note: With any disease you can include head treatment as a part of the disease treatment. In the case of headache, you should very thoroughly treat the place on the head that is aching.

2. Eyes, including all kinds of eye diseases, conjunctivitis, trachoma, leucoma, nearsightedness, trichiasis, ptosis, cataract, glaucoma, etc.,
   1. Eye balls
   2. Inside corners of Eyes
   3. Outside corners of Eyes
   4. Back of the Head

Note: Even though one eye has a problem, treat both eyes. Also treat the kidneys, liver, womb, and ovaries.

3. Ears, Including all kinds of ear diseases, tympanitis, external otitis, ringing ear, hard of hearing, etc.
   1. Auditory canal
   2. Depression just below the ears.
   3. High bone behind the ears.
   4. Back of the Head

Note: Even though one ear has a problem, treat both ears. In the case of diseases which follow colds, such as tympanitis and parotitis, you must treat bronchi, and hilar lymph. Also pay attention to the kidneys, womb, and ovaries.

4. Teeth
   1. In the case of a toothache, treat from the outside of the mouth at the root of the tooth.

5. Oral Cavity
   1. Shut the mouth, and then treat the lips by holding the palms on them.

Note: See Digestive Organs section

6. Tongue
   1. Press on or pinch the diseased part of the tongue.[2]
   2. Treat the root of the tongue from outside the mouth.

Note: If you find this technique difficult, then press both arches of the feet forward.

Digestive Organs

1. Stomatitis
   1. Mouth
   2. Esophagus
   3. Stomach

---

[1] Translated by Midori Eg.

[2] Treating the tongue directly is no longer recommended.

4. Intestines
  5. Liver

2. Thrush
  1. Mouth
  2. Tongue
  3. Esophagus
  4. Stomach
  5. Intestines
  6. Liver
  7. Heart
  8. Kidneys

Note: To heal the tongue, treat the arches of the feet.

3. Saliva
  1. Mouth
  2. Root of the tongue
  3. Stomach
  4. Intestines
  5. Head

4. Esophagus - stricture of the esophagus, dilation of the esophagus, esophagitis
  1. Esophagus
  2. Cardia (solar plexus)
  3. Stomach
  4. Intestines
  5. Liver
  6. Pancreas
  7. Kidneys
  8. Blood exchange*

Note: In the case of esophagus cancer, the prognosis is most likely not very good.

5. Stomach - acute and chronic gastritis, gastric atony, gastric dilation, gastric ulcer, stomach cancer, gastroptosis, neurologic stomach ache, neurologic dyspepsia, gastrospasm
  1. Stomach
  2. Liver
  3. Pancreas
  4. Intestines
  5. Kidneys

  6. Spinal cord
  7. Blood exchange*

Note: If the condition of the cancer is obvious, the prognosis is most likely not very good.

6. Intestine - intestinal catarrh, constipation, appendicitis, vermiform process, ileus, invagination, intestinal volvulus, intestinal bleeding, diarrhea
  1. Stomach
  2. Intestines
  3. Liver
  4. Pancreas
  5. Kidneys
  6. Heart
  7. Blood exchange*
  8. Lumbar vertebrae
  9. Sacrum

7. Liver - Liver congestion, hyperemia, abscess, sclerosis, hypertrophy, atrophy, jaundice, gallstone, etc.
  1. Liver
  2. Pancreas
  3. Stomach
  4. Intestines
  5. Heart
  6. Kidneys
  7. Blood exchange*

Note: A few days after the treatment, gallstones will break into pieces by themselves and will be eliminated from the body. In the case of liver cancer, prognosis is most likely not very good.

8. Pancreas - Liver cyst, ptosis, hypertrophy, etc.
  1. Pancreas
  2. Liver
  3. Stomach
  4. Intestines
  5. Heart
  6. Kidneys
  7. Blood exchange*

Note: In the case of pancreas cancer, prognosis is most likely not very good.

9. Peritoneum
   1. Liver
   2. Pancreas
   3. Stomach
   4. Intestines
   5. Peritoneum area
   6. Bladder
   7. Heart
   8. Kidneys
   9. Blood exchange*

Note: In the case of tuberculosis diseases, treat the lung area.

10. Anal - hemorrhoid, inflammation of anus area, open sores of anus area, bleeding piles, anal fistula, prolapse of the anus
   1. The affected part of anus
   2. Coccyges
   3. Stomach
   4. Intestines

Note: In the case of anal fistula, do the same treatment as intestinal and pulmonary tuberculosis.

Respiratory Diseases

1. Nasal diseases - acute and chronic nasal catarrh, hypertrophic and atrophic nasal catarrh
   1. Nose
   2. Throat
   3. Bronchi

2. Maxillary Empyema
   1. Nose
   2. Depression of upper and front jaw
   3. Chest
   4. Throat
   5. Kidneys
   6. Stomach

7. Intestines
8. Blood exchange*

3. Nosebleed (epistaxis)
   1. Nasal bones
   2. Back of the Head

Note: If menstruation is late and nosebleed occurs, treat the womb and ovaries.

4. Sore throat and tonsillitis
   1. Throat
   2. Tonsil
   3. Bronchi
   4. Kidneys
   5. Lungs
   6. Stomach
   7. Intestines
   8. Head

Note: In the case of tonsillitis, treat the kidneys well.

5. Tracheitis and Bronchitis
   1. Tracheas and bronchi
   2. Lungs
   3. Stomach
   4. Intestines
   5. Heart
   6. Kidneys
   7. Head

6. Pneumonia; catarrhalcroupous
   1. Lungs
   2. Bronchi
   3. Heart
   4. Liver
   5. Pancreas
   6. Stomach
   7. Intestines
   8. Kidneys
   9. Blood exchange*

7. Asthma; chronic and acute asthma
   1. Bronchi
   2. Lungs
   3. Liver

4. Pancreas
5. Diaphragm
6. Stomach
7. Intestines
8. Kidneys
9. Head
10. Nose
11. Heart

Note: In the case of an acute attack, you may let your patient sit up and treat them in this position.

8. Lung - pulmonary edema, abscess, pulmonary tuberculosis, emphysema of lungs.
   1. Lung area
   2. Heart
   3. Liver
   4. Pancreas
   5. Stomach
   6. Intestines
   7. Bladder
   8. Kidneys
   9. Spinal cord
   10. Head

Note: In the case of women regardless of their age, always treat the womb and the ovaries. Doing blood exchange* is effective, but do not do it with very weak or very sick patients.

9. Pleura - both dry and moist
   1. Chest area in general
   2. Heart
   3. Liver
   4. Pancreas
   5. Stomach
   6. Intestines
   7. Kidneys
   8. Blood exchange*

Cardiovascular Diseases

1. Heart - endocarditis, heart valve diseases, various symptoms of pericardium, various symptoms of the heart itself, palpitation, angina pectoris, etc.,
   1. Heart
   2. Liver
   3. Stomach
   4. Intestines
   5. Pancreas
   6. Kidneys
   7. Spinal cord
   8. Blood exchange*

2. Arteriosclerosis - aneurysm, cardiac asthma, etc.,
   1. Same as treating Heart problems
   2. Bronchi and Chest area

Urinary Organ Diseases

1. Kidneys - kidney congestion, anemia, atrophy, sclerosis, hypertrophy, abscess, wandering kidney, pyelitis, kidney stone, uremia, filariasis
   1. Kidneys
   2. Liver
   3. Pancreas
   4. Heart
   5. Stomach
   6. Intestines
   7. Bladder
   8. Head
   9. Blood exchange*

2. Cystitis - urinary retention, uremia, urgency, pain when urinating
   1. Kidneys
   2. Bladder
   3. Urethra
   4. Prostate gland
   5. Womb
   6. Treating same as kidney diseases

3. Enuvesis
   1. Bladder
   2. Intestines

3. Stomach
4. Kidneys
5. Spinal cord
6. Head
7. Blood exchange*

Neurological

1. Cerebral anemia, Cerebral hyperemia
    1. Head
    2. Heart

2. Hysteria
    1. Womb
    2. Ovaries
    3. Stomach
    4. Intestines
    5. Liver
    6. Kidneys
    7. Head
    8. Eyes
    9. Blood exchange*

3. Nervous Breakdown, Insomnia
    1. Stomach
    2. Intestines
    3. Liver
    4. Pancreas
    5. Kidneys
    6. Eyes
    7. Head
    8. Blood exchange*
Note: Be careful with maxillary empyema.

4. Meningitis
    1. Head, mainly back of the head and back of the neck
Note: Mainly treat the head in order to heal the cause of the disease, such as the nose, forehead, and inflammation of the head; also in order to heal remote organs' diseases, such as gastiritis and pneumonia caused by erysipelas. Same for tuberculosis treatment.

5. Epidemic Cerebrospinal Meningitis
    1. Spinal cord
    2. Back of the head and back of the neck
    3. Heart
    4. Stomach
    5. Intestines
    6. Liver
    7. Kidneys
    8. Bladder
Note: Mainly treat the spinal cord, back of the head and back of the neck

6. Myelitis, spinal cord, weakening of the spinal column.
    1. Spinal cord in general
    2. Stomach
    3. Intestines
    4. Liver
    5. Bladder
    6. Kidneys
    7. Head
    8. Blood exchange* (circulation?)

7. Cerebral Hemorrhage, intracerebral bleeding, cerebral thrombosis, etc.,
    1. Head
    2. Heart
    3. Kidneys
    4. Stomach
    5. Intestines
    6. Liver
    7. Spinal cord
    8. Paralyzed area

8. Polio
    1. Spinal cord
    2. Stomach
    3. Intestines
    4. Kidneys
    5. Sacrum
    6. Paralyzed area
    7. Head
    8. Blood exchange*

9. Neuralgia; Palsy, Neural spasticity, Migraine
    1. Affected area
    2. Liver
    3. Pancreas
    4. Stomach
    5. Intestines
    6. Kidneys
    7. Head
    8. Spinal cord
    9. Blood exchange*

Note: Pay attention to the womb and ovaries.

10. Beriberi
    1. Stomach
    2. Intestines
    3. Heart
    4. Liver
    5. Pancreas
    6. Kidneys
    7. Paralyzed or edematous area
    8. Blood exchange*

11. Graves' disease
    1. Womb
    2. Ovaries
    3. Stomach
    4. Intestines
    5. Liver
    6. Pancreas
    7. Heart
    8. Thyroid
    9. Eyes
    10. Kidneys
    11. Spinal cord
    12. Blood exchange*

12. Epilepsy
    1. Liver
    2. Pancreas
    3. Head
    4. Stomach
    5. Intestines
    6. Kidneys

7. Spinal cord
8. Blood exchange*

13. Convulsion
    1. Liver
    2. Stomach
    3. Intestines
    4. Kidneys
    5. Spinal cord
    6. Shoulders
    7. Arms
    8. Elbow joint area
    9. Wrist
    10. Head

14. Chorea
    1. Liver
    2. Stomach
    3. Intestines
    4. Kidneys
    5. Spinal cord
    6. Spastic area at the legs and Arms
    7. Head
    8. Blood exchange*

15. Sea Sick
    1. Stomach
    2. Solar plexus
    3. Head

16. Food poisoning
    1. Stomach
    2. Solar plexus
    3. Liver
    4. Pancreas
    5. Intestines
    6. Heart
    7. Kidneys
    8. Head
    9. Blood exchange*

Infectious Disease

1. Typhoid; Paratyphy
    1. Liver

   2. Pancreas (spleen)
   3. Stomach
   4. Intestines
   5. Heart
   6. Kidneys
   7. Spinal cord
   8. Head

2. Dysentery; Cholera, children's dysentery and others
   1. Stomach
   2. Intestines
   3. Liver
   4. Pancreas
   5. Kidneys
   6. Heart
   7. Head
   8. Blood exchange*

3. Measles
   1. Throat
   2. Trachea
   3. Bronchi
   4. Stomach
   5. Intestines
   6. Heart
   7. Kidneys
   8. Spinal cord
   9. Head

4. Scarlet Fever
   1. Throat
   2. Chest
   3. Kidneys
   4. Stomach
   5. Intestines
   6. Bladder
   7. Head
   8. Blood exchange*

5. Varicella
   1. Stomach
   2. Intestines
   3. Kidneys
   4. Blood exchange*

   5. Affected area
   6. Head

6. Influenza
   1. Nose
   2. Throat
   3. Trachea
   4. Bronchi
   5. Lungs
   6. Liver
   7. Pancreas
   8. Stomach
   9. Intestines
   10. Kidneys
   11. Head
   12. Blood exchange*

7. Whooping Cough
   1. Nose
   2. Throat
   3. Bronchi
   4. Apex of the Lungs
   5. Stomach
   6. Intestines
   7. Kidneys
   8. Blood exchange*

8. Diphtheria
   1. Throat
   2. Trachea
   3. Nose
   4. Lungs
   5. Heart
   6. Liver
   7. Stomach
   8. Intestines
   9. Kidneys
   10. Blood exchange*

9. Malaria
   1. Pancreas (spleen)
   2. Liver
   3. Heart
   4. Stomach
   5. Intestines

6. Kidneys
7. Spinal cord
8. Blood exchange*

10. Tetanus
   1. Jawbone
   2. Back of Head
   3. Throat
   4. Lungs
   5. Affected area
   6. Stomach
   7. Intestines
   8. Kidneys
   9. Spinal cord

Note: In the case of puerperal tetanus, treat the womb. In the case of primary child, treat the navel.

11. Articular Rheumatism, Muscular Rheumatism
   1. Affected area
   2. Heart
   3. Chest
   4. Liver
   5. Pancreas
   6. Stomach
   7. Intestines
   8. Kidneys
   9. Spinal cord
   10. Head

12. Rabies
   1. Affected area
   2. Heart
   3. Liver
   4. Kidneys
   5. Stomach
   6. Intestines
   7. Spinal cord
   8. Throat
   9. Head
   10. Blood exchange*

Whole Body Disease

1. Anemia, Leukemia, Scorbutus
   1. Heart
   2. Liver
   3. Pancreas
   4. Stomach
   5. Intestines
   6. Kidneys
   7. Spinal cord
   8. Blood exchange*

2. Diabetes
   1. Liver
   2. Pancreas
   3. Heart
   4. Stomach
   5. Intestines
   6. Bladder
   7. Kidneys
   8. Head
   9. Spinal cord
   10. Blood exchange*

3. Dermatological Diseases
   1. Stomach
   2. Intestines
   3. Liver
   4. Kidneys
   5. Affected area
   6. Blood exchange*

4. Obesity (Adiposis)
Treat the same as diabetes.

5. Scrofula
   1. Affected area
   2. Stomach
   3. Intestines
   4. Liver
   5. Heart
   6. Chest
   7. Kidneys
   8. Spinal cord
   9. Blood exchange*

Other Diseases

1. Infantile Convulsion
   1. Heart
   2. Head
   3. Stomach
   4. Intestines

2. Syphilis in infants
   1. Affected area
   2. Head
   3. Intestines

3. Wrong position of fetus
   1. Womb

4. Pregnancy
If you treat the womb continually, the growth of fetus will be healthy.

5. Birth of baby
   1. Sacrum
   2. Lumbar spine
Note: If you treat these areas, after twelve labor pains the baby will be born very easily. If you keep on treating these areas after the birth of the baby, the afterbirth will be easy as well.

6. Death of Fetus
If you treat the womb, the dead fetus will naturally come out on the same day or the next day.

7. Cessation of Mother's Milk
If you treat around the breast and mammary gland, the mother will soon start having milk.

8. Morning Sickness
   1. Womb
   2. Stomach
   3. Solar plexus
   4. Intestines

   5. Kidneys
   6. Head
   7. Spinal cord

9. Erysipelas
   1. Affected area
   2. Stomach
   3. Intestines
   4. Liver
   5. Heart
   6. Kidneys
   7. Spinal cord
   8. Blood exchange*

10. Hyperhidrosis
    1. Kidneys
    2. Affected area
    3. Blood exchange*

11. Burn
Put one hand one or two inches away from the Affected area. When the pain is gone, put the hand on this area.

12. Cut by a Sword
Treat as you press the cut with a thumb or a palm to prevent bleeding.

13. Unconsciousness; by falling, or an electric shock, etc.,
    1. Katsu[3]
    2. Heart
    3. Head

14. Drowning
    1. Let the patient throw up water
    2. Katsu[3]
    3. Heart
    4. Head

15. Menopause, Period Pains
    1. Womb
    2. Ovaries

---

[3] Katsu, a technique to revive those who lost consciousness.

3. Cranium

16. Hiccup
    1. Diaphragm
    2. Liver
    3. Pancreas
    4. Kidneys
    5. Stomach
    6. Intestines
    7. Spinal cord
    8. Head

17. Stuttering
    1. Throat
    2. Head
    3. Singing practice

Practice Song
1. Mukou no Koike ni "Dojo" ga sanbiki nyoro-nyoro to. (There are three loaches wiggling in the pond over there.)
2. Oya ga Kahyo nara ko ga Kahyo. Ko-Kahyo ni Mago-Kahyo. (The parent is Kahyo, his child is Kahyo. Son, Kahyo and grandson, Kahyo.) Note: Those who sing songs can be healed.

Editors note: I believe that Dr. Hayashi is saying that singing a song will help those that stutter.

18. Pain at the tip of fingers
    1. Affected area
19. Vomiting
    1. Stomach

2. Solar plexus
3. Liver
4. Spinal cord at the back of Stomach
5. Head
6. Kidneys

20. Splinter
    1. Affected area
Note: When the pain leaves, the splinter comes up. You pull the splinter out at this moment.

21. Gonorrhea
    1. Urethra
    2. Hui-Yin
    3. Bladder
    4. Womb
Note: If it is orchitis, apply your hand lightly on the testicles. (Note that this method is no longer appropriate. Do not touch the genital area.)

22. Spasm of Pain, Stomach Cramps
    1. Stomach
    2. On the back at the stomach
    3. Liver
    4. Kidneys
    5. Intestines
    6. Head

23. Hernia
As you touch the affected area lightly, it will contract by itself.

Treat stomach and intestines.

* Blood exchange, or Ketsueki-Kokan is a technique to get rid of dirty blood, or dirty substances from the body. You stroke along the backbone of the patient from the neck downward. Note from editor: I believe this technique is to release negative energy from the aura of the patient; to avoid doing massage unless you have a license, stroke in the air.

Chapter 7
Hand Positions for Self-Treatment

This chapter and Chapter 9 present the standard hand positions for Reiki treatment. Byosen Scanning, on page 57 and Reiji ho, are other treatment methods in which the aura is treated using hand positions several inches away from the body or one is guided intuitively where to place the hands. You can use either of these methods, or all of them.

In some areas of the country, only licensed medical doctors or nurses or massage therapist may legally touch a client's body. If this is the case and you don't have such a license, use the treatment method shown in Chapter 8.

Position #1

Place your hands over your face with the fingers at the top of the forehead and the hands touching.

Position #2A

Place your hands on the sides of your head over the ears.

73

Position #2B

Place your hands on top of your head with the fingers touching but not overlapping. Palms are close to the top of the ears.

Position #3

Place your hands on the back of your head with the base of the palms at the base of the skull.

Position #4

Place one hand over your throat and the other hand over your heart.

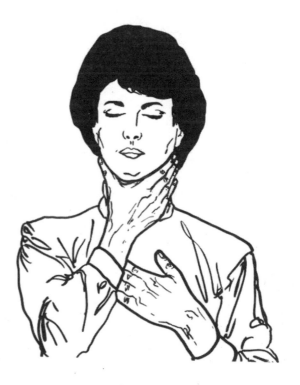

Position #5

Place both hands over your shoulders close to the neck.

Position #6

Place your hands with the fingers touching over the upper stomach just below the rib cage.

Position #7

Place your hands over the middle stomach with the fingers touching at the navel.

Position #8

Place your hands on the lower stomach with the base of the hands near or on the hip bones and the fingertips over the pubic bone.

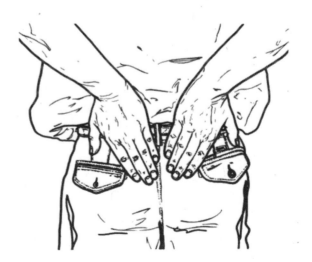

Position #9

Place your hands on the middle back with the fingers touching.

Position #10

Place your hands on the lower back with the finger tips over the sacrum.

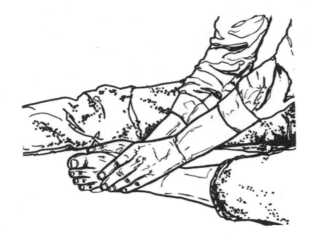

Position #11

Hold your left foot with both hands in a way that is comfortable.

Position #12

Hold your right foot with both hands in a way that is comfortable.

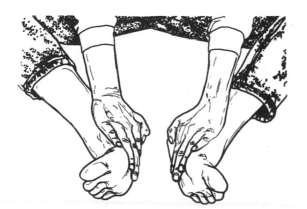

Position #13A

Hold your right foot with your right hand and your left foot with your left hand in a way that is comfortable.

Position #13B

Hold your left foot with your right hand and your right foot with your left hand in a way that is comfortable. This cross over position balances the right and left sides of the nervous system.

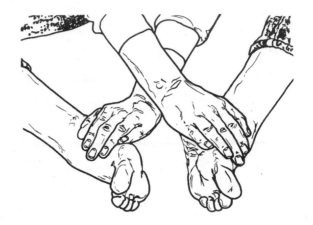

Chapter 8
Alternate Treatment for Self or Others

A complete treatment can be given to yourself or others with the hands one to four inches from the body using the standard hand positions. Because the hands are in the aura, Reiki will treat the aura before it enters the physical body. Illness exists first in the aura before manifesting in the physical body. Treating through the aura will help prevent physical illness from developing in the future.

Reiki energies act in a different, often more powerful way with this technique. They easily travel through the aura to other parts of the energy field, often flowing through and surrounding several areas at once, filling them with warm, loving, nurturing energy before entering the physical body just where they are needed.

Many people find this method to be more effective, while others prefer physical contact. You can use one or the other, or you can mix the two. Simply allow your intuition to guide you in deciding where to use physical contact and where to treat through the aura, or ask the client what he or she prefers.

In some areas of the country, you must be a licensed nurse, doctor or massage therapist in order to legally touch the physical body. Unless you are, it would be better to treat through the aura and avoid hands-on positions. Also, some people do not like to be touched and others suffer from burns or other conditions that are painful to the touch. In such cases, do the complete treatment without touching.

Use this position to beam Reiki to your head, neck, and shoulders. You can direct the beam by changing the angle of your hands. In addition to healing your upper body it will also fill the upper aura with vibrant, healing colors - very powerful!

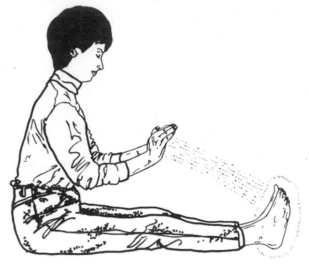

If holding your feet is difficult, beam Reiki to them.

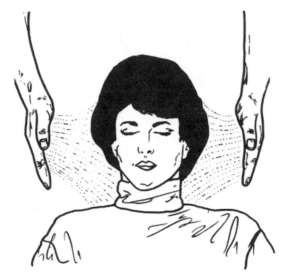

This is similar to position #2A, page 73. Try the other positions and notice the difference.

This position is used to heal the connection between the Crown and Solar Plexus chakras.

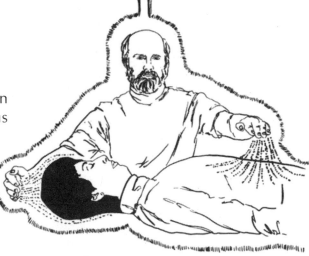

Chapter 9
Hand Positions for Treating Others

The hand positions illustrated in this chapter can be used in place of, or in conjunction with, the aura treatments shown in the previous chapter.

Again, you may need to avoid touching clients in cases like these:

- If the law allows only licensed nurses, doctors or massage therapists to touch clients and you don't have a license of that kind.

- If your client does not like to be touched.

- If your client has burns or any other condition that is painful to the touch.

In all such cases, treat the client through the aura rather than using the hands-on method.

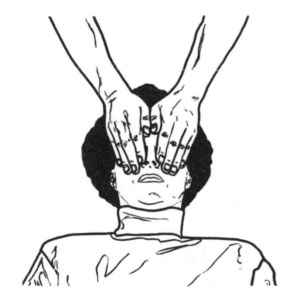

Position #1

Hands are together with thumbs touching. Carefully curve your hands so that the palms do not touch the eyes or eyelashes. Slowly place the base of the hands on top of the forehead with the fingers gently resting on the cheeks. If your hands sweat, place a tissue over the eyes.

Position #2A

Place your hands on each side of the head cupped over the ears with the fingers pointing toward the feet.

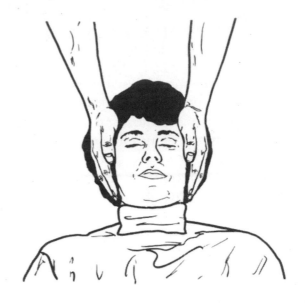

Position #2B

Place the base of your hands together and rest them on the crown of the head with fingers extending toward the ears.

Position #3

Gently cradle the head in your hands. The hands are touching and the fingers are at the base of the skull.

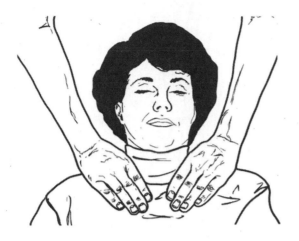

Position #4A

Place your hands over the collarbone with the fingers pointing toward the feet and the thumbs under the neck.

Position #4B

The hands are under the chin and over the throat. One hand is over the other. Use very light pressure and be careful not to touch the throat.

Position #5

Place your left hand under the neck and your right hand over the heart.

Hand Alignment for Abdomen Positions

Place the fingers of one hand at the base of the other hand with either hand on top, whichever is most comfortable.

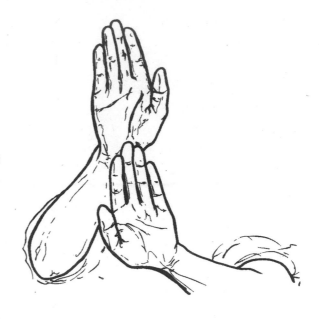

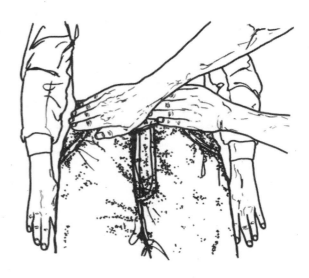

Position #6

Place your hands on the upper abdomen along the ribs.

Position #7

Place your hands on the middle of the abdomen across the navel area.

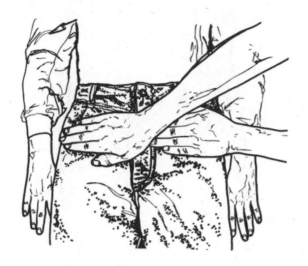

Position #8

Place your hands on the lower abdomen area. Note the hands are placed a little higher than shown to avoid the genitals. You can substitute Torso position 4 shown on page 160

Position #9

Hold the right foot with both hands in a way that is comfortable for you.

Position #10

Hold the left foot with both hands in a way that is comfortable for you.

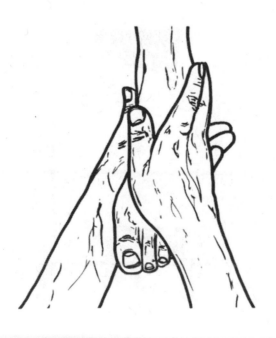

Position #11

Hold both feet in a way that is comfortable for you. You may feel guided to place your palms on the bottom of the feet. If you used three to ten minutes for each position so far, the session will have lasted between forty-five minutes and an hour-and- a-half. You may go to Beaming now, or go on to treat the back. Continue with the back if the client has back problems, or if your intuition indicates to treat the back. Remember: Reiki directs itself and will often flow to places beyond where your hands are positioned. The back often receives Reiki when treating other parts of the body, especially when treating the feet.

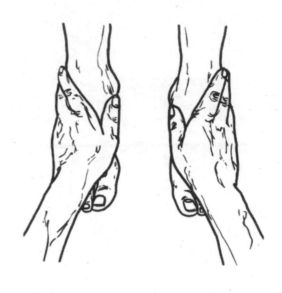

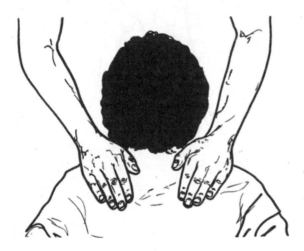

Position #12

Place your hands over the upper back.

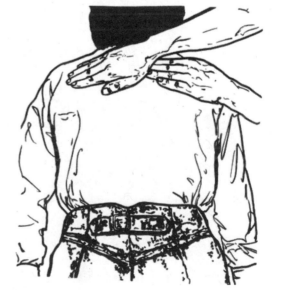

Position #13

Using the same hand alignment for the stomach as illustrated on page 84, place your hands on the upper back.

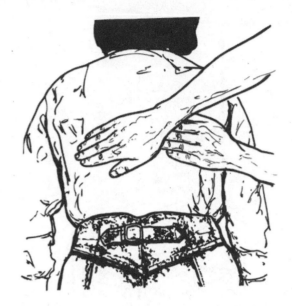

Position #14

Place your hands on the middle back.

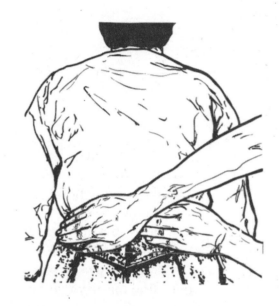

Position #15A

Place your hands on the lower back.

Position #15B

This is an alternate position and can be used if you feel guided to use it. Place your right hand behind the heart and your left hand on the base of the spine. You may also be directed to place your right hand on the crown of the head.

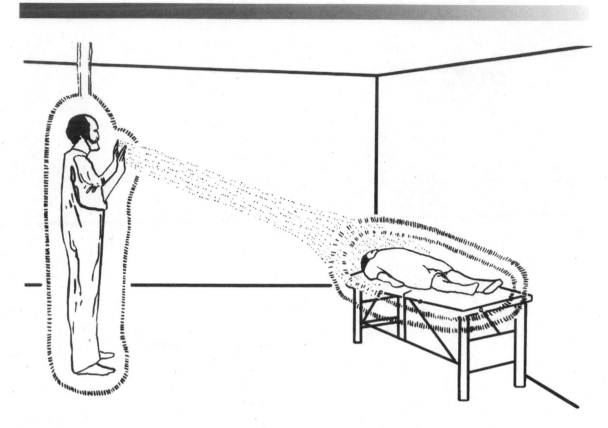

Beaming

At the Center we have developed a powerful method of channeling Reiki energy called Beaming. Using the distant healing symbol it is possible to beam Reiki to your client from across the room. This can dramatically increase the amount of Reiki flowing through you to the client. Beaming also creates a unique healing process of treating the whole aura at once. After treating the aura, the Reiki energy will enter the physical body and treat areas that need it.

It is also possible to beam Reiki directly to a specific area. Just imagine your hands are like radar dishes focusing Reiki on the area you want to treat. You can also direct it with your eyes. Beaming works better if you allow your consciousness to merge with the Reiki consciousness. Simply be aware of the Reiki energy as it flows through you. Focus your mind only on the Reiki. If other thoughts come into your mind, gently brush them away and bring your attention back to the Reiki. By doing this, you will enter an altered state that allows the energy pathways Reiki flows through to open more than normal. It also allows your Reiki guides to more easily add their Reiki to yours. Beaming can be done at the end of a standard treatment or it can be done by itself.

Chapter 10
Giving a Complete Reiki Session

These guidelines are intended to help you organize the various techniques taught in this manual into a complete Reiki session. I suggest when you first begin giving Reiki sessions that you follow them closely. In this way you'll gain experience in the use of a wide range of healing techniques that include the intuitive style practiced in Japan as well as the standard hand placements of Western Reiki.

Before a client arrives do Kenyoku to clear your own energy, then clear and lighten up the energy in the room by burning some sage or using an essential oil. Candles are also helpful and create a nice ambiance.

1. Spend a few minutes talking with your client to gain rapport and to establish the intent of the session. Explain the Reiki process and the various techniques you'll be using and answer any questions the client may have. Ask the client to read and fill out the Client Information Form found at the end of Appendix C.

2. Wash your hands before and after the session. Make sure the client and you are both comfortable during the session. If you sit in an uncomfortable position, it will slow the flow of Reiki. Especially make sure your arms and hands are relaxed. A Reiki table with a chair will make a session more comfortable for you and the client.

3. Before starting the session, ask the client to close his or her eyes and meditate on being thankful for, and open to, all the healing energies that are about to be received. You can also ask the client to focus on and accept any pleasant feelings that develop and to let go of all distress.

4. Let the client know that while it is permissible to talk during the session, it is also appropriate to allow oneself to completely relax.

5. Sit quietly with your hands on your legs doing Reiki on yourself for a few moments. Then draw the power symbol down from the top of your head with the spiral near your root chakra so as to clear, protect, and empower you. You can also draw a smaller power symbol on each chakra starting with the root chakra and going up.

6. Make the power symbol in the middle of the room, and visualize it on the four walls, ceiling, and floor to clear the room of negative energies and fill the room with light. Then say a prayer asking your guides and the client's guides as well as the angels and that of the highest healing forces of the Universe to work with you to protect the process and create the most powerful healing possible.

7. Draw the power symbol on each of your palms, and draw all three symbols over the client's heart, or draw the symbols over the client's

crown chakra imagining them going through the crown and into the heart. As you do this, intend that all the energy from each symbol goes wherever it is needed during the session.

8. Say a short prayer asking that your ego and personal energies be set to the side so that only pure Reiki energy will flow.

9. Do a short Gassho meditation focusing on the space between the palms and releasing all other thoughts. This will strengthen your Reiki energy and get it flowing.

10. Begin the session with Byosen Scanning, which is explained in Chapter 6. By doing this, you will be treating the areas in the aura that are in need of healing. This will create unity in the person's energy field, allowing Reiki to flow more strongly during the hand placements. You may also substitute Reiji-ho and allow yourself to be guided directly to treat those areas most in need of Reiki.

11. Use the complete set of standard hand placements listed in Chapter 9. While placing your hands, use your intuition or the more formal Reiji-ho process to determine when to use the Reiki II symbols explained in Chapter 5 and the Gyoshi-ho and Koki-ho techniques explained in Chapter 6.

12. While using the hand placements, sit quietly, meditating on the relaxing, soothing energies flowing through you. While in this meditative state,

it is also helpful to visualize one of the Reiki symbols that feels most appropriate at that time. Steadily hold the image of the symbol in your mind, gently brushing aside any thoughts that might arise.

13. Be aware that during a Reiki session the client may have feelings come up. This could include feeling sadness and crying, feeling fear and shaking or feeling anger and sweating or there may be other ways that these feelings are expressed. What is usually happening with experiences like this is that old feelings that have been stored in the clients system are awakening so they can be released. Emoting is one way that the release takes place. This is a normal and healthy part of the healing process. If the client begins to cry, or express other feelings, remain calm and continue to give Reiki. Other than offering a tissue if the client is crying there is little else you need to do. The Reiki energy will supply what is needed. Allow the client to continue crying until all the tears are gone. Avoid doing anything that would interfere with the client's emotional expression. If the client cries or emotes longer than 15 minutes or so, ask the client how he or she is doing and if they would like to continue crying or emoting. If you are getting to the end of the allotted time for the session, let the client know this and gently help the client return to present time.

14. At the end of the session, make sure to give Reiki to the client's feet. This will ground the client and bring him

or her back into the body at the same time that it helps integrate the healing that has taken place.

15. End the session by sealing the client's energy field. To do this, draw the power symbol on the client's solar plexus, covering it briefly with your hand and saying to yourself, "I completely seal this Reiki session with divine love and wisdom." Brushing down the aura from the head to the feet also helps to complete the session.

16. Bring the client back slowly. This could include allowing her to lay quietly on the table for a few minutes.

17. Then help her sit up, provide a glass of water if she would like one, and take some time to talk with her about what she experienced.

18. After the client has gone, wash your hands. Do Kenyoku on yourself again, to clear your energy. Then sit quietly doing Reiki on yourself. Visualize the power symbol on the walls and in the center of the room to clear the room. You could also smudge the room to clear the energy after the client has gone.

19. Your Reiki energies will be high at this time so use them for your special projects, distant healing, etc.

Developing Your Own Style

After you have practiced for several months or longer and gain experience in the use of all the techniques in this manual, you may find that because of your unique type of awareness and natural abilities some of the techniques produce better results for you than others. You may also find that Reiki seems to be guiding you to use some techniques more than others. If this begins to happen, and you find that the results you are getting with your clients are improving, then I encourage you to continue to follow your inner guidance. By trusting in yourself and in Reiki and progressing in this way, you'll be making use of your unique abilities and developing your own style as a Reiki practitioner.

On the other hand, some may find that as they continue to follow the steps listed above they develop greater skill in their use which also brings improved results and because of this, will see no reason to vary from them. The amazing thing about Reiki is that it can do no harm and as long as you allow the Reiki energy to do the healing, your sessions will go well regardless of which techniques you use.

Techniques to Enhance the Session

Here are a few additional ideas you can incorporate into your Reiki sessions to empower them, add interest, and make them more therapeutic. You can do all of them or just a few. They can also be used in a self-treatment.

- Have clients write out the things that are not working in their lives. Include all areas of life. (This will cause the problems to come to the surface where Reiki can work more easily on them.) On another piece of paper, have them write out the goals and positive results they would like to achieve. Give them a few minutes by themselves to do this.

- Help them formulate affirmations to heal their problems and achieve their goals. Write the affirmations on another piece of paper. Take all three papers and put them into an envelope, and have your clients hold them durng the session. Be sure to use the mental/emotional symbol during the session to open the subconscious, and draw the symbol with your fingers on each of the papers.

- During the session, have clients repeat the affirmations to themselves. While giving Reiki, imagine you are projecting the affirmations into them. Or both you and the client can repeat the affirmations together out loud while you are giving Reiki and using the Mental/Emotional symbol. Remember, during a Reiki session, clients will be very open to positive suggestion making this a powerful process.

- Make a symbolic ceremony of burning the papers in a metal bowl after the session. If doing this indoors, find a safe place and in any case keep a safe distance. Imagine the flames are transmuting the unwanted conditions into healing and that the goals are being empowered. During the burning, hold your hands toward the flames and have clients do the same. Visualize Reiki symbols in the flames and if clients have had Reiki II, encourage them to join you in the visualization. Have the clients take the ashes home and bury them in their garden. The idea is that the negative things are being buried and composted so the positive things the clients are planting can grow.

Reiki Tables, Chairs and Tools

Providing a comfortable, relaxing setting to give a Reiki session is an important consideration for a Reiki practitioner. Whenever possible, it is best to have a session space that is equipped with a Reiki table for the client and a comfortable chair for the practitioner.

A Reiki table is similar to a massage table: however, a true "Reiki table" is modified slightly with the Reiki practitioner's special comfort needs in mind. Things to look for in a Reiki table are proper height or adjustability, comfortable padding, and Reiki end plates that do not interfere with the practitioner's legs fitting under the ends of the table while seated. A headrest, or face hole are also important features. Please go to www.reikiwebstore.com to see our full line of Reiki tables.

While using a table for a Reiki session is preferable, it is also possible to treat someone while they are seated in a regular chair, a wheelchair, or on a portable massage chair. If you treat a person in a chair, you can simply modify the hand positions to accommodate the situation.

An important thing to remember is that both the practitioner and client should be comfortable during the Reiki session. Reiki is a stress reduction and relaxation technique, and it works best when there is no external tension placed on the body. Taking time to select the proper table can help insure that your Reiki sessions are a pleasant experience for everyone.

Notes

Notes

Part III

Your Own Reiki Practice

The Promise of a Thriving Reiki Practice

People come to you with many different problems, difficulties and illnesses, sometimes as a last resort, and you watch them leave relaxed, often radiant with joy and new hope...seeing them improve over time, watching them grow, gain confidence and become more trusting of life...seeing some make major changes and life adjustments...occasionally witnessing miracles...feeling the wonder of God's love pass through you and into another...sensing the presence of spiritual beings, feeling their touch, and knowing they work with you...being raised into ever greater levels of joy and peace by simply placing your hands on another...watching your life grow and develop as your continual immersion in Reiki transforms your attitudes, values and beliefs...sensing that because of your commitment to help others, beings of light are focusing their love and healing on you and carefully guiding you on your spiritual path. All this is the promise of a thriving Reiki practice!

Chapter 11
Create a Thriving Reiki Practice, Part I
Vision, Intention and Attitudes
This article first appeared in *Reiki News Magazine* (Winter 2006).

If you've taken a Reiki class, even if it is Level I, it's possible to use your skill as a healer to start a Reiki practice. That's right; you don't need to wait until you've become a Reiki Master to start a practice. Back in the 80s, when Reiki II cost $500 and only a select few could become Reiki Masters, it was considered normal and appropriate to start an active Reiki practice after taking the first class. Keep in mind that Takata Sensei worked in Dr. Hayashi's clinic giving professional Reiki sessions to his clients with only Reiki I training.

Remember, you're not the one doing the healing; it's the Reiki energy. Its supply is unlimited, and it is guided by the highest

the time to practice by giving complete sessions with friends and family. If you've taken one of the higher degrees, that is even better, but the important thing is that if you have any level of training, as long as it was good training, you're ready to start right now.

There is tremendous value in having a thriving Reiki practice. Think about what this would look and feel like. If you had 10 clients a week and charged $75 each, you'd be earning close to $40,000 a year just from sessions. You'd likely be working 10–15 hours a week giving the sessions and an additional 10 or so hours for marketing, bookkeeping and other

> *In the development of a thriving Reiki practice, issues, problems and challenges are bound to arise. When this happens, always remember to call on Reiki to guide you through them. There will likely be something within yourself needing to heal.*

Divine wisdom. How could you doubt that it wouldn't work right or provide the healing your clients need? One of the most important lessons the beginning Reiki practitioner or practitioners at any level can learn is to have confidence in the Reiki energy to guide you in creating the healing experience that is exactly right for each client. When you are able to set your ego aside and trust that Reiki will work, you are ready to become a Reiki practitioner. And this can be done even after taking a beginning class! In saying this, I'm talking about someone who has taken a well-organized class from a competent instructor and has also taken

business activities for a total of about 25 hours a week! You'd even be able to work from your home if you wanted to. How do those numbers sound? If you decided to teach, which wouldn't be difficult with that kind of clientele as potential students, you could add an additional $20,000 or more to your income. As you can see, a Reiki practice can be a real job that earns real income. There is also a special satisfaction that comes from being your own boss and running your own business.

In addition to these purely financial results, there are also emotional and spiritual benefits that can be even more fulfilling. You'll be immersed in Reiki energy several hours a day on a regular basis. This will have a positive affect on your health. At the same time, giving Reiki sessions to others and seeing them heal and grow will fill your heart with peace and joy. You'll be providing a service to others and to your community that will connect you to them in a very loving and spiritual way. Being in this type of energetic environment will quicken your personal growth and move you more quickly along on your spiritual path.

As you can see, a successful Reiki practice can provide you with both material and spiritual benefits in a way that is entirely healthy for you and your clients. Getting a successful practice started will require a clear commitment and focused activity over a period of time. Starting out with a part-time effort and eventually working at it full time, it might take six months or more of promoting and developing your practice before you begin to approach the numbers mentioned above, but a thriving Reiki practice provides rewards that are more than worth the effort it takes to create success. Think about how valuable a successful practice will be for you, your life and for those who come to see you for sessions.

The first step toward realizing your goal is to do an assessment of your inner attitudes and beliefs as well as the personal resources you possess that can be employed in the attainment of your goal.

The foundation of all we do is our inner state. It is out of this state that we are able to create what we attempt to do. Having a strong enthusiastic intention to achieve your goal is necessary. If you have a half-hearted desire or are not really excited about creating a thriving Reiki practice, or if you don't really believe you can do it, or if you feel that you don't really deserve it, then you're not likely to do very well. It takes strong motivation backed by emotional energy to achieve a goal as important as this. If you don't have this state spontaneously, or if you find yourself in a slump once you've started your project, there is something you can do to pump yourself back up. Here's an exercise that is important to do right from the beginning and continue every day. It will give you the energy and enthusiasm you need to accomplish your goal.

Goal Manifesting Exercise

1. Write your goal on a 3x5 card something like this: "I have a thriving Reiki practice. I see ten or more clients a week and teach classes. I have a thriving Reiki practice. I see ten or more clients a week and teach classes. I have a thriving Reiki practice. I see ten or more clients a week and teach classes." Be sure to repeat it three times.
2. Then place the card in your hand. If you've taken Reiki II or higher, draw all your Reiki symbols in the air over the card. If not, then simply use Reiki by itself.
3. Place the card between your hands and give it Reiki, intending that the Reiki energy empower and manifest your goal.
4. As you do this, repeat the affirmation to yourself over and over as you send it Reiki.
5. In addition, visualize yourself with a thriving Reiki practice. Picture this imagery in a field of Reiki light up above your head. See yourself

looking at your client file and seeing it full of client records. See checks and money flowing into your pocket and your bank account. See yourself in your treatment room working with a client knowing many more are on the way. When you visualize this, know in your heart that when this happens, it will be a truly exciting and satisfying accomplishment. Fill yourself with feelings of excitement, joy and success as though it's actually happening right now! Allow yourself to get caught up in this inner state so that you lose awareness of your surroundings and are as fully absorbed as possible in the positive feelings of having a thriving Reiki practice.

6. Do this exercise at least once a day, but more often if possible. The more you do it, the better you'll be able to enter the desired state and the more beneficial it will be for you.

This exercise is very important to practice everyday. It is part of the training you need to strengthen your energy field and cultivate the inner qualities necessary to excel at accomplishing your purpose. It is better if you do it at the same time each day, such as in the morning before you start your day or at lunchtime. Not only will it give you the personal energy to accomplish your goal and motivate you to do what you need to do, it will enhance your creativity and create a powerful magnetic force that will attract to you all the people and resources you need. This will make it much easier to develop a thriving Reiki practice.

Because Reiki energy is the basis of this process, you'll be developing a special connection to the highest level of guidance and healing. This connection will develop over time to be a wonderful source of strength, inspiration and encouragement that will help you develop all the personal qualities necessary to accomplish and even surpass your goals.

Business Consciousness

Since Reiki is a spiritual practice, some of you may have a feeling, either consciously acknowledged or lurking around in the subconscious, that spiritual things and the material world don't belong together. If this feeling is present, it needs to be dealt with and healed. There is nothing wrong with the spiritual and material working together. In fact, that's the whole purpose for spiritual beings (you and me) to be in material bodies—to bring the values and energy of the spiritual world into the material world. Having a spiritual business is an excellent way to accomplish this purpose.

Often a person may be a great healer but does not do well because he or she hasn't taken the time to develop the necessary business skills. In fact some practitioners actually shun the business aspect and then complain that they aren't making any money. This doesn't make sense. Remember, if you charge money for what you do and what you do is helping others, the better your business operates, the more people you'll be able to help, and this will directly affect your income. So don't shy away from the fact that you charge money and that you are a business person. You need to fully embrace it and be the best business person you can be.

Remember, regardless of your current knowledge or skill level, you can always improve. So even if you don't think you have the aptitude, it's important to take the time to learn and get the business aspect of your operation set up as well as you can. Some basic things you'll need are a set of books to record income and expenses and a marketing program. I'll discuss more about this in Part II of this article.

In setting up and operating your Reiki business, it's important to keep the spiritual and material in balance and working together in harmony. In your business practices, always make sure you are honest and fair in all you do and that your primary motivation is to sincerely help your clients. As your income goes up, you'll be able to expand your program and provide more services, thus helping even more people.

Money Issues

Since you're charging money for Reiki sessions and classes, your relationship to money will have a lot to do with how successful you become. Our culture seems to have a love-hate relationship with money. Remember, money is not good or bad in itself. It's no different than any other tool you might have. Think of a match. A match can be used to light a fire to cook your food or to burn down a house. Money is the same way. It's not what money is that counts, but what you do with it. If you earn your money honestly by providing services that people value and if you save and spend it wisely, then you'll be using money in a healthy way that is in alignment with the energy and principles of Reiki.

Since money is a major issue for most people, it's important for you to look at how you feel about money and heal any issues that come up. Here are some thought experiments. Try them out. You may not get negative feelings from these exercises, but if you do, it's important to think about and heal them by including the issues in your regular self-healing sessions.

Money Thought Experiment

1. How do you feel when you find out someone else might be making more money than you?
2. How do you feel when you realize that you're making more money than someone else?
3. Think about how much money you're making right now. Then think what it would be like to make twice as much or three times as much. Do you feel like you are balancing on the top of a pole, afraid you're going to fall off? Are you afraid some one is going to take your money from you or that it will be difficult to hang onto?

If you want to have a successful Reiki business, it's important for you to be connected to money in a healthy way that empowers you to establish your spiritual values in the material world. If the above thought exercises bring up unhealthy feelings, or if other experiences with money cause unhealthy feelings, it's important that you acknowledge them and heal them. Doing this will create the necessary foundation for you to live a healthy and prosperous life.

Competition

An issue that is likely to come up in your Reiki practice is competition from other Reiki practitioners. Your understanding and your attitude toward competition will play an important role in how you deal with it and how it affects your Reiki practice. Fear of competition has caused more problems and restrictions for Reiki practitioners than any other issue. This fear is based on the illusion that there isn't enough for everyone, that another Reiki teacher will take your clients or students or that if there are too many Reiki practitioners in your area, then you'll have fewer clients. Remember, FEAR is really False Evidence Appearing Real. This is especially true for Reiki. It is the fear of competition that causes problems, not competition itself.

It's important to always maintain a healthy, positive attitude toward other Reiki practitioners and teachers. If you fear them or are jealous of them or have other negative feelings toward them, then your vibration will be lowered and this will cause you to attract fewer clients. Fear of competition tends to be self-fulfilling.

There is an important lesson about this topic we can learn from Reiki. Reiki energy comes from an unlimited supply. Because of this, we'll never run out of Reiki energy, no matter how many people are giving Reiki sessions. The reason Reiki is unlimited is that it comes from a higher level of consciousness. As long as we come from a higher level of consciousness when we plan and carry out our business activities, we'll be able to tap into this same unlimited supply, which will result in abundance and prosperity in our lives.

Remember, potential Reiki clients and students are sensitive to energy. They also know that Reiki is a spiritual practice. They are looking for a practitioner/teacher who has a high vibration and who lives by spiritual values. If you have negative feelings toward other Reiki practitioners,

potential customers will easily detect your attitude, and they'll tend not to be attracted to you. This will also happen subconsciously, as those interested in Reiki usually have a higher intuitive sense and will be guided away from those with a lower vibration. Therefore, it's important for you to deal with any negative feelings that come up within you and heal them. Always say positive things about other Reiki people or say nothing at all.

Reiki is guided by the highest spiritual wisdom, and it also works in other ways by guiding clients and students to the right teacher. Those who are on spiritual paths or who are seeking healing often receive help from spirit guides who are on the lookout for the right Reiki practitioners for them. Therefore it's important to maintain a high spiritual vibration and to have the attitude that no one can take students or clients away from you, and you're not taking them from other Reiki practitioners, but that all students and clients are guided to the teacher or practitioner that is right for them. This will keep you in alignment with the Reiki energy and with the highest spiritual forces that are guiding the healing community.

It's also important that the primary motivation for your Reiki practice be to truly help your clients and students. If you are overly focused on money or have a need to control others, prospective clients/students will notice this, and they will not be attracted to you. Their spirit guides will recognize this attitude even more readily and will be less likely to guide them to you. Because of this, it's really important to be clear about your motivation. A good question to ask yourself is why you want to have a thriving Reiki business. While there may be a number of good reasons, the primary one that will really work is that you truly want to help people.

Some Reiki teachers have attempted to get their students to sign non-competitive agreements indicating that they won't teach in their territory. Others have declared that a certain area is their territory and that other teachers can't practice there. Again, this tactic is based on fear and ends up having the opposite affect than what was intended. The teacher usually ends up with less business because the energy of fear and control repels potential students and clients. Also, it's important to think in terms of how Reiki might think of a situation like this. If Reiki is focused on providing benefit to the client or student, wouldn't it be better if clients and students had more choices for potential teachers and practitioners? If you're in a situation where you're being told that you're in someone else's territory, send Reiki to the situation and follow the guidance you receive. Make sure that you respond in a way that maintains your high vibrational state and honors the values of Reiki. Remember, unless some prior agreement has been made, there are no territories in the Reiki world.

It's been found that when Reiki teachers and practitioners work together to promote Reiki, rather then competing with each other, they create a vortex of positive energy that is a much stronger attractive force than each of them working separately. This was demonstrated by Laurelle Shanti Gaia and Kathie Lipinski while they were practicing Reiki in Louisville, Kentucky. (See "Creating Harmony in the Reiki Community" in the Reiki Articles section at www.reiki. org) They organized teachers in their area who were competing with each other

in negative ways and got them to work together in harmony. This may seem like a daunting task, but they called on Reiki to help and had the courage to follow their guidance. It worked! Because their group, called *United In Healing*, had so many members, they were able to organize events they wouldn't have been able to create on their own. They networked with support groups for breast cancer, fibromyalgia, diabetes and other chronic illnesses. They sponsored Reiki marathons for critically and chronically ill people and had a free clinic. In one weekend, their members had over 102 students in Reiki classes. This was a real blessing to the teachers and especially to the students and the community.

If you maintain a positive mental attitude toward members of the Reiki community in your area, your connection to Reiki will remain strong, which will allow the wisdom of Reiki to continue guiding you. This will make it easy to meditate with Reiki requesting insight on how to manage your business and how to improve it so as to attract more business, so that rather than competing, you can focus on creating. Remember, the purpose of Reiki and of your Reiki business is to provide benefit to your clients and students. If you're not getting the results you'd like, then place your focus on creating greater benefits for your clients and students. Develop your Reiki practice by taking more training to enhance your healing abilities, improving your teaching skills and the way your classes are organized, revising and upgrading your class manuals, promotional brochures, and website, or develop new teaching aids and marketing ideas. This is the positive way to deal with competition: improve your business.

In the development of a thriving Reiki practice, issues, problems and challenges are bound to arise. When this happens, always remember to call on Reiki to guide you through them. There will likely be something within yourself needing to heal. As you heal and release your inner issues, the outer issues will be resolved as well. This is the miracle of Reiki. As you focus on helping others you also benefit. And as this process unfolds, your Reiki business can turn into an important part of your spiritual path.

Part II will focus on practical ways to develop and market your Reiki practice. Before reading part II of this article I suggest you read this article again and practice the Goal Manifesting Exercise and the Money Thought Experiment along with really using the ideas in this article and giving yourself Reiki for any issues that come up. By doing so you'll have strengthened your foundation and be ready for the practical application that I'll be sharing with you in part II.

Whatsoever thou resolveth to do, do it quickly. Defer not till the evening what the morning may accomplish.

—Unto Thee I Grant

Notes

Create a Thriving Reiki Practice, Part II

This article first appeared in *Reiki News Magazine* (Spring 2007).

Part I of this article (Winter 2006) focused on developing your state of mind. This is the most important part of creating a thriving Reiki practice because everything you create originates in your mind. The quality of the thoughts and feelings that surround your goals determines your likelihood of achieving them. The clearer you create your images of success and the stronger you believe in them, the more directly you'll be manifesting your goals with your mind. To say it another way: the mind is like a broadcasting station, sending out a signal that tells the Universe what to create for you. If you believe that creating a Reiki

techniques and methods presented here have been tested and proven to work. But you must understand that each person and each situation is different and may require a unique combination of these methods or the development of methods not mentioned here.

Here is a formula for success. If followed carefully, it will guide you to the achievement of your goals.

1. Clearly decide on your goal. This must be stated in a concrete way using numbers and dates. As an

The Secret of Success

I began saying a prayer right after I received my Reiki I training. I said this prayer sincerely everyday. It guided me to be a Reiki master and inspired me to develop my Reiki practice. It has continually created miraculous results in my life. The prayer is: **Guide me and heal me so that I might be of greater service to others.**

practice will be hard and that you're not likely to get many clients, this is what the Universe will create for you. On the other hand, if you believe that creating a thriving Reiki practice will be easy and that you're going to have an abundant number of clients, then this is what the Universe will create for you. This is the inner marketing aspect of your business, and *it must come first*. Only by believing in yourself and the worthiness of your goals will you be able to convince others to do the same. So, if you haven't read Part I, I suggest you read it and put into practice the exercises it contains.

Assuming you are developing your inner marketing program, you can now start your outer marketing program. The ideas,

example, you might decide your goal is to average 10 Reiki clients per week within four months.

2. Develop a plan and follow it. Remember – those that fail to plan, plan to fail. Base your plan on methods others have used to achieve similar goals. The methods mentioned in this article are a good place to start. Remember to meditate with Reiki energy when contemplating the use of a particular method and in developing your plans. Reiki will guide you in miraculous ways and open doors you didn't know were there.

3. As you implement your plan, keep a record of the results you get. Note what methods work best to move

you toward your goal. Also note which ones don't work or produce poor results. It is important not to guess; keep records and look at the numbers.

4. Keep doing the things that work. Stop doing the things that don't work.

5. By eliminating the things that don't work, you'll have additional time and resources. Use them to try new things.

This may appear to be a very simple formula—because it is. Achieving success isn't a complicated process. It's just a matter of doing the right things consistently until you reach your goal. Note that even though it's a simple formula, each step is important and must be followed. As you follow this plan, over time you will develop a powerful set of business practices that move you toward your goal quickly and efficiently.

Reiki Room

You'll need a place to give your Reiki sessions. You can use a room in your home or rent an office. An office gives a more professional appearance and is a demonstration of your commitment. It is an additional business expense, but it can be cost effective by attracting more clients. However, if you can't afford it at the beginning or if you're guided to do so, it's also possible to set up a room in your home to give sessions.

You will need a Reiki table, a CD player, a couple of chairs, a table and a small filing cabinet for your records. Soft lighting, candles and incense are often helpful to create ambiance. The more relaxing and comfortable your Reiki room is, the more receptive your clients will be to the healing work you do.

Liability Insurance

I've never heard of anyone being sued for a bad Reiki session, but liability insurance can still be a good idea in some situations. Professional liability insurance will protect you if for some reason the client claims he or she was harmed by the Reiki session. The insurance company will legally represent you and negotiate with the client or defend you in court if necessary (even though this is unlikely to happen). However, the main reason to have it is that it is required by hospitals and medical clients if you should get the opportunity to give Reiki sessions there. While you usually won't receive pay for volunteering in a hospital or medical clinic, you will gain quality experience that will strengthen your professional credibility, enhance your bio, and likely increase the number of clients you have in your regular Reiki practice. It is also tremendously rewarding on an emotional and spiritual level.

General liability insurance is different from Professional liability insurance and is important for you to have. It will protect you if your client should fall off your Reiki table or if he or she slips and falls in your home or on the driveway in front of your home or in some other way becomes injured while on your property.

The Reiki Membership Association offers an excellent Reiki insurance program that includes both Professional and General liability for multiple modalities at an excellent price. Find out more at: http://www.reikimembership.com/Insurance.aspx or see page 174.

Records

There are various records you'll need to keep. These include:

1. Client records: I suggest using the Client Information Form that you can download free from our Website: http://www.reiki.org/Download/FreeDownloads.html. This form informs the client that Reiki does not take the place of medical treatment. It is also a way to keep track of client contact information, as well as keeping a session history so you can check progress and see what techniques you have used and their results. It is also a way to collect email addresses for your email list, which is an important way to market your business.
2. Bookkeeping records: This can start out simply with a record book to keep track of expenses and income. You will also need a file for keeping expense receipts. You will need these for tax purposes, but it is also important to keep records to track the performance of your business and check your progress toward your goal.

Business Expenses are Tax Deductible

Because you are operating a business, you will be able to deduct business expenses from your income taxes, for which you will need records. Office rent, training expenses, including travel and lodging, as well as electricity, heat, gas for your car, and so forth may all be deducted from your taxes.

As your business expands, you may find it easier to use a computer accounting program. There are several that are free,

such as Microsoft Accounting Express 2007, and others, such as Intuit or QuickBooks, that charge a fee. Besides making your bookkeeping easier, they usually include other helpful features such as a contact manager that will allow you to create a list of all your clients and contact people and which usually includes an email list manager.

Marketing Tools

You need to promote your business by letting people know who you are and the services you offer. There are many ways to do this, and it is important to try as many as possible and track the results you get from each, so you can keep doing what works and stop doing what doesn't.

It is possible to start your Reiki business on a shoestring, and this may be the best way for many to get started, but at some point, it will be necessary to increase the amount of money you spend on marketing and promotion. This can be done gradually. As you get more clients, your income will grow, and it will be possible to expand your marketing program proportionally. When spending more on promotion, it's important to carefully track your results so you can keep doing the things that are cost effective and stop doing those that aren't. At the same time, it's important to keep in mind that there are many ways to promote your business that don't involve a lot of expense.

Email List

One of the most effective things you can do to promote your Reiki practice is develop an email list of those interested in Reiki. In today's world people use email to communicate far more than snail mail. This is because email is easy, fast and inexpensive. If you're promoting your Reiki practice, it's easier to compose an email and send it to your email list than to mail a flyer. With email, it's as easy as clicking a mouse button a few times, and it's done with almost no expense. With snail mail, it will take hours or days to get the mailing ready, and the expense can be in the hundreds or even thousands of dollars. Email is the way to go and results are almost instantaneous.

Because of this, it's important to begin collecting email addresses of those interested in Reiki right away. Collect them from your clients by having them fill in their email addresses on your Client Information Form and collect them from all the promotions and events you're involved with.

You can use your email list to remind people about your Reiki practice, let them know about promotions or special deals you have, or about your Free Reiki Evenings or Fund Raisers and so forth. *An effective email list is the most important marketing tool you can develop.*

Many email software programs allow you to send to a large list without the whole email list going to each recipient. There are bulk email websites that provide online software for sending out to large lists, and you can also get your own software programs and install them on your computer or on your Web server. Do a Google search for Bulk Email Service to locate providers. One email program I recommend is Subscribe Me Pro http://www.siteinteractive.com/subpro/ This program is only $59.00 and provides tracking.

To learn more about the importance of email for marketing I suggest you go to the Guerrilla Marketing website at www.gmarketing.com and read their article on email and marketing. You will also find other interesting articles there. I recommend you order the book, Mastering Guerrilla Marketing, which explains how to achieve your marketing goals with minimum expense.

Web Site

While a website isn't a necessity and you can start your Reiki practice without one, it's important to get a website as soon as possible to take advantage of its important marketing features. A website is a handy way to let people know what you do. Rather than trying to give a detailed verbal description of your services to people, or give them a bunch of handouts, just give them your web address. They will have access to all of your material and be able to read through it at their leisure and return again and again until they convince themselves to come to you for a session. Also, the Web is such an integral part of society now that if you don't have a website, most people will think you're not serious about your business.

A well-designed Reiki website needs to contain:

1. An explanation of Reiki, including a Frequently Asked Questions section.
2. A description of your sessions, how long they last, your fee, etc. Testimonials from your clients are also a big plus.
3. If you're teaching, include a class schedule and a complete description of what each class contains, and what students will be able to do after

taking each class. Class fees and prerequisites should also be listed.

4. A bio of yourself including a picture and especially your training background and experience.

5. Articles you have written about Reiki.

6. An email collection box to collect email addresses of visitors to your site.

7. Contact information including phone, email address, city and state, but not your home or business street address. Your exact location, including a map, can be sent separately to those who have scheduled a session or signed up for a class. This will prevent people from coming by without an appointment.

You can start out with a simple site that you design, but after a while, it's a good idea to have a professional webmaster design and set up your website. Remember that people will determine who you are by the quality of the promotional material you provide. So make sure your website looks professional, is well organized, clearly communicates your ideas and provides useful information. One way to find a good webmaster is to find websites online that you like and contact the webmasters of those sites to find out how much they charge for web design, and get a feel for whether you can work with them, etc.

As I mentioned above, an important feature for your website is an email collection box. This provides a method for you to collect the email addresses of those who frequent your website. Subscribe Me Pro provides a method of setting this up. To get people to give you their email address, you'll need to offer them something. You could offer to give them a podcast or recording of a Reiki talk or meditation you've recorded or to receive a free Reiki newsletter or something of that nature. Be sure to place a value on what they'll get such as $5 or $10.

Business Cards

It's important to have a business card listing your name, phone and, especially, your email address and website, along with your business name, if you have one, and the Reiki services you offer. It's better not to list your street address to prevent people from coming to your office without an appointment. A business card lets people know you're serious and professional and makes it easy for people to contact you. Carry them with you at all times. You will be surprised at the number of opportunities to pass out your cards, especially when you're focused on the promotion of your Reiki practice.

Short Explanation of Reiki

Create short, succinct answers for basic Reiki questions so you'll be ready to explain Reiki to those who express interest. When people ask what Reiki is, I usually say; *"Reiki is a Japanese technique for relaxation that also promotes healing. It's done through touch. A warm and soothing energy flows from the hands into the client, promoting relaxation and releasing tension."* This answer usually inspires comments such as: "I could really use something like that." Or "Boy do we really need that around here." If you get a positive response like this, offer to give a short demo of five minutes or so to treat the person's shoulders or anywhere they may have tension or an ache or pain. Then give them a business card and answer any other questions they may have. They may contact you for a session or may refer others.

Impromptu Reiki Sessions

When you're out and about, talk to people, and weave the fact that you do Reiki into your conversation. If they ask what Reiki is, give them the short explanation above and offer to give them a short demo. Just place your hands on their shoulders to show them how the energy feels. Often they'll say things like, "I really need this," or "Wow that's going right for my sore arm," or "My headache is going away." Or you may be talking to someone and they mention an ache or pain they have. Immediately offer to give them Reiki for it. Many times, they'll already know what Reiki is, or if not, then give them your short explanation. Then let them know you do professional Reiki sessions and give them your card. You could also go on to explain how Reiki can help those undergoing chemotherapy and how it promotes healing after surgery and so forth. A hands-on experience like this will leave an impression, and even if they don't sign up for a session, they may refer others to you. Most will know of someone going into the hospital or in need of healing for one condition or another.

This technique is great at parties. You can either weave into your conversations that you do Reiki or those you talk with may offer that they have an ache or pain or a tense situation at work, which is a great lead-in for offering them Reiki. Once you start giving a demo session, often a crowd will gather, and you can give a little talk about Reiki to those watching as you give the treatment. Afterwards, pass out your business cards to those interested.

Upward Price Technique

If you are just starting a Reiki practice, try this technique for motivating people to come to you for sessions. When someone asks how much you charge, say, "I'm giving 10 sessions for free, and I've already given four (or whatever the number is at that point). Then say, "After the 10 free sessions, I'm going to be charging $10.00 per session." This will motivate people to sign up right away so they get a free session and avoid having to pay $10.00. After you've given out your 10 free sessions when someone asks how much you charge, say, "I'm giving 10 sessions for $10 each, and I've already given three (or whatever the number is at that point). After the 10, my price is going up to $20 per session." This will continue to motivate people to get sessions from you while the price is low. Continue with this process until you reach your target fee. By working like this, you'll be charging a fee based on your experience, and you will be motivating people to come to you quickly for sessions so they will save money.

Target Fee

Your target fee is the fee you want to work up to for Reiki sessions after you've gained experience, developed your business and have a steady stream of clients. Your target fee will vary depending on the part of the country you live in. Doing a little research will help you figure this out. One way is to check with other experienced Reiki practitioners in your area to see what they charge. Another way is to set your target fee in the same range as professional massage therapists are charging in your area. Also remember that additional factors to consider when determining your target fee are the amount of training you've had, the amount of experience and the results clients get from your sessions.

Clients Are Your Best Promoters

Those who have experienced your work are the best people to promote you. Make sure you give every client some of your business cards to hand out to friends, family and acquaintances who could use Reiki sessions.

Bonus Program

Creating a bonus program based on clients getting free sessions for bringing you new paying clients is also a way to promote your practice. When you give your clients business cards to pass out, tell them that for every two paying clients they send to you, you'll give them a free session. When clients come to you, you'll need to ask them how they found out about your practice and if anyone referred them to you. Use an Excel spreadsheet to keep track of how many each client referred to you. When a client gets the required number, email them and let them know they've earned a free session. Concerning the number they need to get a free session, remember that the idea is to build up your Reiki practice quickly and that each new client could become a promoter of your business too. Keeping the required number low will motivate them to work harder promoting your business.

Professional Referrals

Make friends with the chiropractors, massage therapists, acupuncturists, aroma therapists, medical doctors and other professionals in your area and let them know that you'll refer clients to them, if they'll refer clients to you. Collect business cards from them and give each some of yours. If they are hesitant to do this, offer them a free session, and then give them some of your cards to give to their clients. This method can also open the possibility of being offered a job giving sessions at a clinic.

Flyers

It's good to have a basic flyer to promote your business. Carry them with you to place on bulletin boards in health food stores, bookstores, churches, and so forth and to give to prospective clients. Include a brief explanation of Reiki and the benefits it provides. If possible, include testimonials from your clients. Also be sure to create special flyers to reflect new promotions or services you're offering.

Magazine Advertising

I would be leaving out an important marketing method if I failed to mention advertising in the *Reiki News Magazine*. The magazine goes directly to 20,000 people who have a serious interest in Reiki, and it's a fact that those who advertise in our magazine get results. This is especially true for those who provide professional advertising copy and graphics and advertise regularly. If you want to find the ads that are working, check the current issue and then work your way through previous issues to see who's advertising consistently. The ads that appear in multiple issues are the ones that are working because people don't continue advertising unless it is cost effective.

Free Reiki Evening

This is also called a Reiki Share group and is an evening usually offered on a regular basis, such as once or twice a month, when Reiki practitioners get together to exchange Reiki. People who have never experienced Reiki can also be invited. Those who have Reiki training are asked to bring their Reiki tables. Usually a talk is given at the beginning that explains Reiki and answers questions. Usually, those new to Reiki receive sessions first, often with several practitioners giving them Reiki at the same time. A table can be set up for practitioners to display their business cards and flyers. Announcements about classes or other Reiki activities can also be made. Include a registration sheet to get names and email addresses to add to your email list so you can keep them notified about future Reiki events.

This is an excellent way to meet new Reiki practitioners, attract those seeking healing and to advertise your practice. A subtle benefit of these meetings is that it keeps Reiki awareness high in your community and creates good will that will come back to you to support your practice. See "How to Create a Successful Reiki Share" in the summer 2014 issue of *Reiki News Magazine*.

Fundraisers

Non-profit organizations such as churches and charity groups often sponsor fundraising events. You could volunteer to set up and operate a Reiki fundraising event to benefit a group you wish to support. In this event, you provide free Reiki sessions and the clients give either a donation or a fixed fee to the organization. Be sure to create a sign-up sheet that includes the recipient's email address so you can add them to your email list. Explain on the sign-up sheet that you may use their email address to let them know about other Reiki events. Operating a Reiki fundraiser will give

you valuable experience and enhance your professional reputation. You will also have the satisfaction of helping a group you believe in at the same time you're helping those who receive your Reiki sessions. Once the event is over, you're likely to get people wanting to come to you for additional Reiki sessions. See The Saga of a Reiki Fundraiser on page 32 of the Spring 2007 issue of *Reiki News Magazine* for more information.

Holistic Fairs

Getting a booth at a holistic fair can be another effective way to promote your Reiki practice. Get several Reiki practitioners to help you. Take a Reiki table, a sign and plenty of business cards and flyers. Offer ten or fifteen- minute Reiki sessions for $10 and have three or more Reiki practitioners giving the sessions to each person. Create a sign-up sheet that includes the recipient's email address. It's possible to generate income at the same time you promote your Reiki business.

These are a few of the many ways you can promote your Reiki business. As you try these ideas, and especially if you follow the manifesting meditation practice in Part I of this series, you'll come up with additional ways that are just right for you. As you move forward and achieve your goal, you'll experience the miracle-working power of Reiki manifesting abundance in your life. Usui Sensei said, "Reiki is the secret art of inviting happiness." Certainly you will experience a great happiness as you create a thriving Reiki practice. May you always be blessed by the radiant light of Reiki.

Chapter 12
Becoming a Reiki Master

In the end, we must consider that the process of becoming a Reiki Master is not a process in which we master Reiki, but one in which we allow Reiki to master us.

Reiki is a sacred practice that requires reverence and our greatest respect if we are to experience its full value. The benefits of Reiki can be all-encompassing, not only giving us the ability to heal ourselves and others, which by itself is deeply meaningful, but also bringing guidance for our lives. Its unlimited nature can create opportunities for continual growth and unfoldment of our boundless potential. The ever increasing joy, peace and abundance that await those who sincerely pursue the path of Reiki are not only a blessing to be enjoyed, but also contain the healing the planet so dearly needs. Those who have been initiated into Reiki often feel this greater potential and aspire to continue to the Advanced and Master levels.

The desire to grow is inherent in simply being alive. As we look around ourselves and observe other living things, we can clearly see that all living things share the impulse to grow. Because this is what living things do, one could even say that the purpose of life is to grow and develop. Therefore, the desire to grow in one's Reiki potential is a natural expression of one's core essence and of life itself. If you feel this desire in your heart, honor and respect it. Doing so will fulfill an innate need.

Reiki - A Joyful Path

The joys of becoming a Reiki Master are many and you don't necessarily have to teach in order for the Master training offered by the Center to be useful. The additional healing energy, symbols, techniques and knowledge will add value to your healing abilities. Treating yourself and treating others in person and at a distance will all be noticeably improved. The fact that you can pass Reiki on to friends and family is also a definite plus. Many take the Master training with just this in mind. However, if you ever decide to formally teach, you will be able to do so. As you take the Center's Reiki Master training and increase your personal vibration, this adds to the vibration of the whole planet!

One of the greatest joys of Reiki Mastership is teaching Reiki to others. Imagine the thrill of witnessing the members of your Reiki class receiving Reiki energy during the attunement and then, as you guide them in its use, sharing in their joy and amazement as they experience its gentle power flowing through them for the first time. As your students use Reiki to help family, friends and clients, a wonderful sense of spiritual connection will develop among all of you. Feelings of compassion and love for everyone will be strengthened as you merge with the Reiki consciousness and know more deeply than ever before that we all come from God and that we are all one in God.

What Is a Reiki Master?

The definition of a teaching Reiki Master according to the Center is anyone who has received the Master attunement and master symbol and who understands how to give all the attunements. In order to be considered a Reiki Master, one must also have taught Reiki to at least one other person. Those who have taken Reiki Master training but not taught Reiki to anyone would not qualify as Reiki Masters so far as the Center is concerned and should call themselves Reiki Master practitioners instead until they do begin to teach.

Master Training Is a Serious Step

Becoming a Reiki Master is a serious step that requires definite preparation. One must first take Reiki I & II and Advanced Reiki Training. Practice using Reiki is absolutely necessary. Experience with the energy and using the symbols is a must. It is also necessary to meditate on your life purpose and decide if Reiki Mastership is in harmony with it. Then, it is important to study with a competent and compatible Reiki Master who will encourage and help you after you become a Reiki Master.

How to Find the Right Teacher

Before taking Reiki Master training, you should ask your prospective teacher exactly what you will be able to do after you are trained. Will you receive the complete training and be able to initiate others into all the degrees including full Reiki Master? Or will something be left out, requiring you to take additional sublevels or degrees and pay additional fees? Because of changes some have made to the system of Reiki, this is a very important question to ask. If you choose to study with one of the Center's Licensed Teachers, you will receive the complete Reiki Master training.

Becoming a Reiki Master implies the ability to initiate others into Reiki.

Therefore, it is important to find a teacher who will spend time in class helping you practice the attunement processes used in the initiations. Ask potential teachers how much time is spent in class practicing the attunements, as some teachers spend little or none. Also ask them how much support they are willing to give you to begin teaching your own classes. This is important. Some Reiki Masters will have little interest in helping you get started, as they are afraid you will take students away from them. If you are serious about becoming a successful teaching Reiki Master, find a teacher who will openly support you in achieving your goal.

After taking the Master training and before teaching your first class, additional practice doing the attunements is a good idea. This can be done on friends who already have Reiki. Ask them if they would like to be "attunement models" and let them know that the additional attunements will be beneficial for them and will refine and strengthen their Reiki energies. Most will gladly agree. If you can't find someone to practice on, you can use a teddy bear or a pillow to represent a person.

It will also be necessary to practice the talks, lectures and meditations you will be leading in class. Make outlines of your talks and practice reading them into a recorder. Listen to your recordings and take notes on ways you can improve your talks. Then continue to practice until you are confident. Don't be afraid to use your outline in class. When teaching, relax and let the Reiki energy do the work.

If you have a sincere desire to help others and have taken the time to prepare, you should have no trouble attracting students.

It is your attitude that creates the results you receive, so assume success and you will create success.

Treat Students with Great Respect

As a teaching Reiki Master it is important to treat your students with the greatest respect. Know that all have the spark of God within them. Never use subtle threats or withhold information to make your students dependent on you. Openly encourage all students to be connected to their own power and freedom of choice. What you create for others comes back to you. As you truly empower others, so will you be empowered. Trust in the abundance of the Universe and you will receive abundance. You will also be blessed with peace and joy.

Set a Good Example

When teaching Reiki to others, it is important to set a good example by being an authentic representative of Reiki energy. People cannot be so easily fooled by surface spirituality now. They want and need a real teacher who comes from experience and is working on her or his own deep healing. This requires one to meditate on the nature of Reiki energy and surrender to it. It is a continual process of working with all aspects of one's being that are out of step with Reiki energy and allowing the energy to heal them. We must seek to develop and express the qualities of love, compassion, wisdom, justice, cooperation, humility, persistence, kindness, courage, strength and abundance, as Reiki energy is all of these and more. It may seem paradoxical, but it is true that a real Reiki Master is one who is always becoming a Reiki Master. Like life itself, it is a process of continual growth.

As you do this, you will realize sooner or later that there is more to Reiki than using it to heal yourself and others of specific problems. Reiki has a deeper purpose. In the same way that Reiki is able to guide healing energy when you are giving a treatment, Reiki can guide your life.

Your Life Purpose

There is a perfect plan for your life that has always been present and waiting for you. This plan is exactly what is good and right and healthy for you. This plan is not necessarily based on what your parents want for you, or what the culture says you need to do to be accepted. It is based on your inner potential that longs to express and therefore on what will really make you happy. This plan is inside of you and comes from your core essence. Reiki can activate and help you follow this plan, which is your true spiritual path.

By treating yourself and others and by meditating on the essence of Reiki, you will be guided more and more by Reiki in making important decisions. Sometimes you will find yourself doing things that don't seem to make sense or conform to what you think you should be doing, and sometimes you will be guided to do things that you have told yourself you would never do. However, by trusting more and more in the guidance of Reiki, by letting go of what your ego thinks it needs to be happy and by humbly surrendering to Reiki's loving power, you will find your life changing in ways that bring greater harmony and feelings of real happiness.

The Way of Reiki

Over time, you will learn from experience that the guidance of Reiki is worthy of

115

your trust. Once you have surrendered completely, you will have entered *The Way of Reiki*. When you do this, you will be at peace with the past, have complete faith in the future and know that there never was anything to worry about. Your life will work with ever greater harmony, and you will feel that you have reached your goal of wholeness even as you continue to move toward it!

In the end, we must consider that the process of becoming a Reiki Master is not a process in which we master Reiki, but one in which we allow Reiki to master us. This requires that we surrender completely to the spirit of Reiki, allowing it to guide every area of our lives and become our only focus and source of nurturing and sustenance.

The Way of Reiki offers itself as a solution to our problems and as a path of unlimited potential. May all who would benefit from this path be guided to it.

Notes

Notes

Notes

Notes

Appendices

Appendix A

Discovering the Roots of Reiki

Discovering the Roots of Reiki

by William Lee Rand and Laurelle Shanti Gaia

As teachers and practitioners of Reiki we have enjoyed sharing the "traditional" story of the history of Reiki as it has been taught to us in the West. However, this story has never felt complete to us, and many others have told us they felt the same way. Important information seemed to be missing, and parts of the story didn't seem to fit. Some of the "facts," upon investigation, proved to be untrue, and much of·the rest of the story could not be verified.

The information available in the West about Dr. Usui, or Usui Sensei as he is called by Reiki students in Japan, has been so limited and larger-than-life that some people have wondered if he ever really existed at all. This has made it difficult to feel connected to him and to the roots of the system he created.

In 1996 we published an article on the "Original Reiki Ideals" which revealed a more authentic version of the ideals we had been given in the West. Since then, additional information has been uncovered from the investigations of Japanese Reiki researchers and others. The most interesting and verifiable of this new information is from Frank Arjava Petter in his new book, *Reiki Fire*. Arjava was one of the first Western Reiki Masters to teach other Masters in Japan, which he began in 1993.

Japanese Sources for Reiki History

With the help of his Japanese wife Chetna and Japanese Reiki Master Shizuko Akimoto, Arjava contacted a number of people who have proved to be important sources of information about the history of Reiki. Two of these, Tsutomo Oishi and Fumio Ogawa,[1] learned Reiki from a Master who had been taught by Usui Sensei himself. Arjava also spoke to members of Usui Sensei's family and to members of the Usui Reiki Ryoho Gakkai, the original Reiki organization started by Usui Sensei in Tokyo. From these contacts he filled in some missing information on the history of Reiki and discovered other valuable facts. This information provides more accurate insight into who Usui Sensei was, what motivated him to discover Reiki and how he and his students practiced.

After reading Arjava's book, we were interested in knowing more and e-mailed him with many questions. He answered our questions and invited us to Japan to visit the sacred sites and discuss the implications of this new information. We gladly accepted and flew to Japan the second week of September 1997.

Our Trip to Japan

Many synchronicities occurred in connection with our trip to Japan, starting with someone faxing us important pages from Arjava's book. Before and after our trip was scheduled, we met people who lived in Japan who offered to act as additional guides for us.

Just two weeks after we met on the Internet, Friedemann Greulich traveled

---

[1] The lineage of both Fumio Ogawa and Tsutomo Oishi is the same: Mikao Usui, Iichi Taketomi and Keizo Ogawa. Iichi Taketomi eventually became the president of the Usui Reiki Ryoho Gakkai. Keizo Ogawa was a good friend of Usui Sensei's and also received his Reiki Master initiation from him.

from Japan to the University of Kentucky on business and visited Laurelle at her Healing Center in Kentucky to exchange Reiki sessions. At this time we had not planned our trip to Japan. It turned out that Friedemann lives only 10 minutes from where Arjava lives in Japan and he offered to help us at Mt. Kurama!

Another person, Yuki Yamamoto, flew from Osaka to the Center to attend a Karuna Reiki® class, knowing nothing about our planned trip. Osaka is close to Mt. Kurama and Yuki had been there many times. When he found out about our trip, he offered to join us at Mt. Kurama with his car and be our guide.

So, without seeking it, we had several extra guides that proved to be very helpful! We feel these things happened as a result of our daily Reiki practice during which we invite the energy to guide every aspect of our lives.

Mt. Kurama - Where Reiki was Discovered

According to literature at the Mt. Kurama Temple, in 770 A.D. a priest named Gantei climbed Mount Kurama, led by a white horse. His soul was enlightened with the realization of Bishamon-ten, the protector of the northern quarter of the Buddhist heaven and the spirit of the sun. Gantei founded the Buddhist Temple on Mt. Kurama which went through many stages of development and restoration and now contains many temples and pagodas. The temple was formerly part of the Tendai sect of Buddhism. Since 1949, it has been part of the newly founded Kurama-Kokyo sect of Buddhism.

Arjava, Yuki and Friedemann accompanied us to Mt. Kurama during our several trips to the mountain. (Pictures from our trip appear on pages 27-31.) Mt. Kurama has wonderful energy! The Kurama Temples are located up the side of the mountain, requiring that one hike up and down the mountain to visit them. This would normally be very tiring, but we found that taking a moment to rest there quickly restores one's energy. Mt. Kurama is truly a "power spot" and the energy that flows is very uplifting, yet calming. There is a feeling of contentment and peace. We both were aware of many helpful spirits from whom we received inspiration and guidance.

Our first stop up the mountain was at the San-mon Station. There is a shrine here representing the Trinity which, in the Kurama-Kokyo Buddhist sect, is known as Sonten or Supreme Deity. Sonten is thought to be the source of all creation - the essence of all that is. Sonten is said to have come to Earth over six million years ago in the form of Mao-son, the great king of the conquerors of evil, who descended upon Mt. Kurama from Venus. His mission was the salvation and evolution of mankind and all living things on earth. Mao-son is also said to have incarnated as the Spirit of the Earth, residing inside an ancient cedar tree at the top of the mountain. This spirit is thought to emanate from Mount Kurama to this day. Sonten manifests on Earth as Love, Light and Power.

Roots of the Reiki Symbols

The love symbol is called Senju-Kannon and looks very similar to the Usui mental/emotional symbol. It is the Sanskrit seed syllable *hrih*. The light symbol is called Bishamon-ten and is represented by the Sanskrit seed syllable *vai*. The power symbol is called Mao-son and is represented by the Sanskrit seed syllable *hum*. The essence of all three is in each one. It is interesting to note the similarity between these three symbols and the symbols of Reiki II. Pictures of these symbols appear on pages 27-28.

The kanji for the Usui master symbol is also used in the Kurama Temple literature. The meaning of Sonten is expressed using the same kanji we use for the Usui master symbol. During a temple prayer in the Hondon Temple, we were given special permission to be present as the priest used the name of the Usui master symbol during part of his chant!

It has to be more than a coincidence that the Usui master symbol is used by the Kurama Temple to represent Sonten, the Supreme Deity, and that the symbol which represents love looks very similar to the Usui mental/emotional symbol. Since Usui Sensei received his Reiki initiation on Mt. Kurama, it is likely he made use of some of the symbolism and philosophy of the Kurama Temple in the formulation of Reiki.

In fact, the understanding we received from Shizuko Akimoto is that Usui Sensei studied many things before discovering Reiki. He took what he studied and combined what seemed right into the Usui System of Healing. This is apparent in the "Original Reiki Ideals" which we now know came from the Meiji Emperor. This is indicated in the inscription on the Usui Memorial, located at Saihoji Temple. The inscription also indicates Usui Sensei studied many things, but his life was not going well when he decided to go to Mt. Kurama to meditate for answers. Perhaps he was looking for the kind of personal transformation for which the mountain is noted and for help in healing his life. It seems he did what many of us have done when our

lives have not gone well and we have looked to the spiritual for answers and healing. He opened himself to the Higher Power and not only received a healing for himself, but a way to help others.

Mt. Kurama is covered with giant cedar trees. As we hiked upward, we passed through a section of the trail near the top of the mountain covered with roots, and we thought, yes, the roots of Reiki. At the top of the mountain there is a quiet place with a small shrine called Okunoin Mao-den where Mao-son is said to have descended. Behind the shrine protected by an iron fence is the old cedar tree said to contain the spirit of Mao-son. This area is very calm and has the sound of running water and wind blowing through the trees. We spent a long time here meditating and giving Reiki treatments and attunements to each other.

The Usui Memorial - Answers Carved in Stone

With the help of Arjava Petter, we found the memorial dedicated to Usui Sensei, the founder of the Reiki healing system. It is located at the Saihoji Temple in the Suginami district of Tokyo. The memorial was created by the Usui Reiki Ryoho Gakkai in 1927, shortly after Usui Sensei's transition, and is still maintained by the Usui Reiki Ryoho Gakkai. This was verified by officials of the Saihoji Temple where the memorial is located. We were surprised that the Usui Reiki Ryoho Gakkai still exists because part of the "traditional" story was that all the members of this group died in the war or had stopped using Reiki and that Mrs. Takata was the only remaining teacher of the Usui system in the world. We now know the Usui Reiki Ryoho Gakkai has always existed since Usui Sensei's time and it still exists today.

The memorial consists of a large monolith about four feet wide and ten feet tall. On it, written in old-style Japanese kanji, is a description of Usui Sensei's life and his discovery and use of Reiki. It is located in a public cemetery at the Saihoji Temple next to Usui Sensei's gravestone where his ashes, along with those of his wife and son, have been placed. The inscription on the memorial stone was written by Mr. Okata, who was a member of the Usui Reiki Ryoho Gakkai, and Mr. Ushida, who became president after Usui Sensei died. There are many important and interesting details included in the inscription. (See Chapter 1.)

We went to the memorial site with flowers and we burned some sage there. A butterfly came and landed on the flowers we brought and it felt very peaceful as we drew all the Usui Reiki symbols and sent Reiki to Usui Sensei. We held hands and prayed for Reiki and Usui Sensei to guide us in writing this and sharing a more accurate understanding of Reiki worldwide. We asked for this new information to help unite all Reiki practitioners in harmony and to inspire them to use Reiki to heal each other, all people of the world, and the Earth as a whole. While meditating, we became aware of Usui Sensei with a bright light all around him. We felt he was very happy that an image of his memorial would be seen by so many and that a clearer understanding of how he practiced Reiki would become known.

In Japan Fees for Treatment Are Optional

Shizuko Akimoto shared additional information about Usui Sensei and the history of Reiki. According to her research with Fumio Ogawa and other members of the Usui Reiki Ryoho Gakkai, there was never a mandatory fee for Reiki treatments. Dr. Hayashi charged whatever people could pay and if they were poor, he treated them for free. His Reiki business was not lucrative, but was done out of a desire to help people. Many of his students received their Reiki training in return for working at his clinic. If Usui Sensei became popular helping people who suffered from the Tokyo earthquake, as it states on his memorial, it is likely that he, too, did not insist on everyone paying a fee for his treatments but, like Dr. Hayashi, must have treated many for free.

There is no title of "Grand Master" or "Lineage Bearer" in the organization started by Usui Sensei.

The high fees for Master training charged by some in the West are not a requirement of the Usui Reiki Ryoho Gakkai. Also, Usui Sensei and Dr. Hayashi are known to have given out class manuals to their students, thus removing another obstacle to learning Reiki - the requirement of a perfect memory! We have received a copy of one of Dr. Hayashi's Reiki manuals and have translated it. It is a description of various illnesses and the hand positions to treat them.

Since Reiki was not a lucrative business, some of Dr. Hayashi's students were forced to stop practicing Reiki due to a lack of adequate income. This suggests that a middle financial path may be more appropriate. A middle path allows one to charge reasonable fees so that one can earn a living, yet be able to lower fees when appropriate or charge nothing for those unable to pay. This allows people to dedicate their life to doing Reiki fulltime, thus creating more adept healers who are able to help a greater number of people.

The Lineage of Usui Sensei

According to Arjava Petter, there is no title of "Grand Master" or "Lineage Bearer" in the organization started by Usui Sensei. The person in charge of the Usui Reiki Ryoho Gakkai is the president. Usui Sensei was the first president of the organization. Since then, there have been six successive presidents: Mr. J. Ushida, Mr. Ilichi Taketomi, Mr. Yohiharu Watanabe, Mr. Toyoichi Wanami, Ms. Kimiko Koyama and the current president is Mr. Kondo who accepted the office in 1998. Dr. Hayashi was a respected teacher, but was never president.

Language and cultural differences along with reluctance on the part of the Usui Reiki Ryoho Gakkai to speak with Western Reiki practitioners has restricted our communication. This is why information about the original Usui Reiki organization has taken so long to surface in the West. However, some communication has occurred and a breakthrough is expected soon as the inscription on the Usui Memorial states it is Usui Sensei's wish that Reiki be spread throughout the world.

Helping Others Is What Reiki is All About

This new information about Reiki confirms what many of us have intuitively known all along - the main focus of Reiki is to help others, and because of this there is no need to always require payment for treatments or for training if the person is in need and unable to pay. Mandatory high fees for the teaching level are not a requirement. Moreover, Reiki was not always an oral tradition and both Usui Sensei and Dr. Hayashi had written materials they gave to their students.

Attunements and the practice of Reiki were originally based more on intuitive guidance and intention than on set rules, with the Reiki energy being the defining element. The flexibility of the Usui system makes it broad enough to include a wide range of methods and techniques, thus validating the many different styles being practiced today. We believe the leadership for Reiki lies in Japan where it originated, not in the West.

The Usui Memorial, the information it contains and the energy of Mt. Kurama provide us with an enduring legacy that unites us with Usui Sensei and the spirit of Reiki he discovered. This connects us to the roots of the Usui system and to the living energies of its origin. The Usui Memorial with its inscription can provide a focal point for all Reiki groups and a common link that can help to heal the fragmentation and competitiveness which have developed in the West.

Indications of other important discoveries have also made themselves known. These include written materials from Usui Sensei and others. More open communication is likely to occur with members of the Usui Reiki Ryoho Gakkai including the president, and is bound to reveal additional useful information. This is the most wonderful time for Reiki in the West now that we are finally learning the real story of Reiki. Many are feeling a wonderful sense of coming home. May we all share in the joy of these new discoveries and allow them to inspire and empower our Reiki practice.

Notes

Appendix B

Reiki in Hospitals

Reiki in Hospitals

William Lee Rand

At hospitals and clinics across America, Reiki is beginning to gain acceptance as a meaningful and cost-effective way to improve patient care. Personal interviews conducted with medical professionals corroborate this view.[1] "Reiki sessions cause patients to heal faster with less pain," says Marilyn Vega, RN, a private-duty nurse at the Manhattan Eye, Ear and Throat Hospital in New York. [Reiki] accelerates recovery from surgery, improves mental attitude and reduces the negative effects of medication and other medical procedures.

Vega, a Reiki master, includes Reiki with her regular nursing procedures. Because the patients like Reiki, she has attracted a lot of attention from other patients through word of mouth, as well as from members of the hospital staff. Patients have asked her to do Reiki on them in the operating and recovery rooms. She has also been asked to do Reiki sessions on cancer patients at Memorial Sloane Kettering Hospital, including patients with bone marrow transplants. Recognizing the value of Reiki in patient care, 6 doctors and 25 nurses have taken Reiki training with her.

America's Interest in Complementary Health Care

The general public is turning with ever-increasing interest to complementary health care, including Reiki. In fact, a study conducted by Dr. David M. Eisenberg of Boston's Beth Israel Hospital found that one in every three Americans has used such care, spending over 14 billion out-of-pocket dollars on alternative health care in 1990 alone![2]

A survey conducted in 2007 indicates that in the previous year 1.2 million adults and 161,000 children in the U.S. received one or more energy healing sessions such as Reiki.[3]

Reiki is also gaining wider acceptance in the medical establishment. Hospitals are incorporating it into their roster of patient services, often with their own Reiki-trained physicians, nurses and support staff. Reiki was in use in hospital operating rooms as early as the mid-90's.[4] Since then its acceptance in medicine has grown. It is now listed in a nursing "scope and standards of practice" publication as an accepted form of care,[5] and a 2008 USA Today article reported that in 2007 15% of U.S. hospitals (over 800) offered Reiki as a regular part of patient services.[6]

---

[1] The comments that follow were part of an interview I did with each person either in person or by telephone and were first published in my article, "Reiki In Hospitals," which appeared in the Winter 1997 issue of the *Reiki Newsletter* (precursor to *Reiki News Magazine*).

[2] Eisenberg, David, et al. "Unconventional Medicine in the United States," *New England Journal of Medicine* 328, no. 4 (1993): 246–52.

[2] Beth Ashley, "Healing Hands", *Marin Independent Journal*, May 11, 1997.

[3] P. M. Barnes, B. Bloom, and R. Nahin, CDC National Health Statistics Report #12. *Complementary and Alternative Medicine Use Among Adults and Children, United States*, 2007. (December 2008).

[4] Chip Brown, "The Experiments of Dr. Oz," *The New York Times Magazine*, July 30, 1995: 20–23.

[5] American Holistic Nurses Association and American Nurses Association (2007), *Holistic Nursing: Scope and Standards of Practice* (Silver Spring, MD: Nursesbooks.org.)

[6] L. Gill, "More Hospitals Offer Alternative Therapies for Mind, Body, Spirit," *USA Today*, September 15, 2008 (Online) http://www.usatoday.com/news/health/2008-2009-2014-alternative-therapies_N.htm.

For a detailed description of 64 Reiki hospital programs, please go to www. centerforreikiresearch.org

Scientific Validation

A research study at Hartford Hospital in Hartford, Connecticut indicates that Reiki improved patient sleep by 86 percent, reduced pain by 78 percent, reduced nausea by 80 percent, and reduced anxiety during pregnancy by 94 percent.[7]

In 2009, The Center for Reiki Research completed the Touchstone Project, which summarized Reiki studies published in peer-reviewed journals. The 25 studies examined were further evaluated to determine the effectiveness of Reiki. The conclusion states: "Overall, based on the summaries of those studies that were rated according to scientific rigor as "Very Good" or "Excellent" by at least one reviewer and were not rated as weak by any reviewer, 83 percent show moderate to strong evidence in support of Reiki as a therapeutic modality."[8]

Why Hospitals Like Reiki

Hospitals are undergoing major changes. They are experiencing a need to reduce costs and at the same time improve patient care. Under the old medical model based on expensive medication and technology this posed an unsolvable dilemma. Not so with Reiki and other complementary modalities. Reiki requires no technology

at all and many of its practitioners offer their services for free. Reiki is therefore a very good way to improve care while cutting costs.

Julie Motz, a Reiki trained healer has worked with Dr. Mehmet Oz, a noted cardiothoracic surgeon at Columbia Presbyterian Medical Center in New York. Motz uses Reiki and other subtle energy techniques to balance the patients' energy during operations. She has assisted Dr. Oz in the operating room during open heart surgeries and heart transplants. Motz reports that none of the 11 heart patients so treated experienced the usual postoperative depression, the bypass patients had no postoperative pain or leg weakness; and the transplant patients experienced no organ rejection.[9]

An article in the Marin Independent Journal follows Motz's work at the Marin General Hospital in Marin County, California, just north of San Francisco.[10] There Motz has used subtle energy healing techniques with patients in the operating room. She makes a point of communicating caring feelings and positive thoughts to the patients, and has been given grants to work with mastectomy patients in particular.

Dr. David Guillion, an oncologist at Marin General, has stated "I feel we need to do whatever is in our power to help the patient. We provide state of the art medicine in our office, but healing is a multidimensional process. . . . I endorse the idea that there is a potential healing that can take place utilizing energy."

---

[7] "Hartford Hospital, Integrative Medicine, Outcomes," http://www.harthosp.org/integrativemed/outcomes/default.aspx#outcome6. Measurements cited were obtained during the initial pilot phase of the study, December 1999–December 2000.

[8] The Center for Reiki Research, Touchstone Project, Conclusion, http://www.centerforreikiresearch.org/RRConclusion.aspx.

[9] Julie Motz, *Hands of Life* (New York: Bantam Books, 1998).

[10] Ashley, "Healing Hands."

Reiki at Portsmouth Regional Hospital

Patricia Alandydy is an RN and a Reiki Master. She is the Assistant Director of Surgical Services at Portsmouth Regional Hospital in Portsmouth, New Hampshire. With the support of her Director Jocclyn King and CEO William Schuler, she has made Reiki services available to patients within the Surgical Services Department. This is one of the largest departments in the hospital and includes the operating room, Central Supply, the Post Anesthesia Care Unit, the Ambulatory Care Unit and the Fourth Floor where patients are admitted after surgery. During telephone interviews with pre-op patients, Reiki is offered along with many other services. If patients request it, Reiki is then incorporated into their admission the morning of surgery, and an additional 15-20 minute session is given prior to their transport to the operating room. Some Reiki has also been done in the operating room at Portsmouth Regional.

The Reiki sessions are given by 20 members of the hospital staff whom Patricia has trained in Reiki. These include RN's, physical therapists, technicians and medical records and support staff. Reiki services began in April 1997, and as of 2008 have given 8000 Reiki sessions.

"It has been an extremely rewarding experience," Alandydy says, "to see Reiki embraced by such a diverse group of people and spread so far and wide by word of mouth, in a positive light. Patients many times request a Reiki [session] based on the positive experience of one of their friends. It has also been very revealing to see how open-minded the older patient population is to try Reiki. In the hospital setting Reiki is presented as a technique which reduces stress and promotes relaxation, thereby enhancing the body's natural ability to heal itself."

The Reiki practitioners do not add psychic readings or other new-age techniques to the Reiki sessions, but just do straight Reiki. Because of these boundaries, and the positive results that have been demonstrated, Reiki has gained credibility with the physicians and other staff members. It is now being requested from other care areas of the hospital to treat anxiety, chronic pain, cancer and other conditions.

Alandydy, with her partner Greda Cocco, also manage a hospital-supported Reiki clinic through their business called Seacoast Complementary Care, Inc. The clinic is open two days a week and staffed by 50 trained Reiki volunteers, half of whom come from the hospital staff and the rest from the local Reiki community. They usually have 13-17 Reiki tables in use at the clinic with 1-2 Reiki volunteers per table. The clinic treats a wide range of conditions including HIV, pain, and side-effects from chemotherapy and radiation. Some patients are referred by hospital physicians and some come by word of mouth from the local community. They are charged a nominal fee of $10.00 per session. The clinic is full each night and often has a waiting list.

The California Pacific Medical Center's Reiki Program

The California Pacific Medical Center is one of the largest hospitals in northern California. Its Health and Healing Clinic, a branch of the Institute for

Health and Healing, provides care for both acute and chronic illness using a wide range of complementary care including Reiki, Chinese medicine, hypnosis, biofeedback, acupuncture, homeopathy, herbal therapy, nutritional therapy and aromatherapy. The clinic has six treatment rooms and is currently staffed by two physicians, Dr. Mike Cantwell and Dr. Amy Saltzman. Cantwell, a pediatrician specializing in infectious diseases, is also a Reiki Master with training in nutritional therapy. Saltzman specializes in internal medicine and also has training in mindfulness meditation, acupuncture and nutritional therapy. Other professionals are waiting to join the staff, including several physicians.

The doctors at the clinic work with the patients and their referring physicians to determine what complementary modalities will be appropriate for the patient. A detailed questionnaire designed to provide a holistic overview of the patient's condition is used to help decide the course of treatment. The questionnaire involves a broad range of subjects including personal satisfaction with relationships, friends and family, with body image, and with job, career, and spirituality. The clinic is very popular and currently has a waiting list of more than 100 patients.

Dr. Cantwell provides 1-3 hour-long Reiki sessions, after which he assigns the patient to a Reiki II internist who continues to provide Reiki sessions outside the clinic. Patients who continue to respond well to the Reiki treatments are referred for Reiki training so they can continue Reiki self-treatments on a continuing basis.

Dr. Cantwell states: "I have found Reiki to be useful in the treatment of acute illnesses such as musculoskeletal injury/pain, headache, acute infections, and asthma. Reiki is also useful for patients with chronic illnesses, especially those associated with chronic pain."

At this point, Reiki is not covered by insurance at the clinic, but Dr. Cantwell is conducting clinical research in the hope of convincing insurance companies that complementary care is viable and will save them money.

More MD's and Nurses Practicing Reiki

Mary Lee Radka is a Reiki Master and an R.N. who has the job classification of Nurse-Healer because of her Reiki skills. She teaches Reiki classes to nurses and other hospital staff at the University of Michigan Hospital in Ann Arbor. She also uses Reiki with most of her patients. She has found Reiki to produce the best results in reducing pain and stress, improving circulation and eliminating nerve blocks.

Reiki Master Nancy Eos, M.D., was a member of the teaching staff of the University of Michigan Medical School. As an emergency-room physician, she treated patients with Reiki along with standard medical procedures.

"I can't imagine practicing medicine without Reiki," Eos says. "With Reiki all I have to do is touch a person. Things happen that don't usually happen. Pain lessens in intensity. Rashes fade. Wheezing gives way to breathing clearly. Angry people begin to joke with me."

In her book Reiki and Medicine she includes descriptions of using Reiki to treat trauma, heart attack, respiratory problems, CPR, child abuse, allergic reactions and other emergency-room situations. Dr. Eos now maintains a family practice at Grass Lake Medical Center and is an admitting-room physician at Foote Hospital in Jackson, Michigan, where she continues to use Reiki in conjunction with standard medical procedures. According to Dr. Eos, there are at least 5 other physicians at Foote hospital who have Reiki training along with many nurses.[11]

Libby Barnett and Maggie Chambers are Reiki masters who have treated patients and given Reiki training to staff members in over a dozen New England hospitals. They teach Reiki as complementary care and the hospital staff they have trained add Reiki to the regular medical procedures they administer to their patients. Their book Reiki Energy Medicine describes their experiences.[12] One of the interesting things they recommend is creating hospital "Reiki Rooms," staffed by volunteers, where patients as well as hospital staff can come to receive Reiki treatments. Bettina Peyton, M.D., one of the physicians Libby and Maggie have trained states: "Reiki's utter simplicity, coupled with its potentially powerful effects, compels us to acknowledge the concept of a universal healing energy."

Anyone interested in bringing Reiki into hospitals is encouraged to do so. The hospital setting where there are so many people in real need is a wonderful place to offer Reiki. The experiences and recommendations in this article should provide a good starting point for developing Reiki programs in your area.

*Editors Note: *It is very important when giving Reiki treatments in hospitals or otherwise to make sure the patient understands what Reiki is and to only provide a Reiki treatment if the patient has requested one. Also, if the issue comes up, it is important to explain that while Reiki is spiritual in nature, in that love and compassion are an important part of its practice, it is not a religion and that members of many religious groups including many Christians, Muslims, Hindus and Jews use Reiki and find it compatible with their religious beliefs.*

---

[11] Nancy Eos, *Reiki and Medicine* (Eos, 1995).

[12] Libby Barnett and Maggie Chambers, with Susan Davidson, *Reiki Energy Medicine* (Rochester, Vermont: Healing Arts Press, 1996).

Notes

Appendix C

Reiki Training and the ICRT Reiki Membership Association

Reiki I and II

Reiki I and II are taught together during a two day weekend intensive. All attunements are given. All the information and techniques in this manual are covered including:

- ✿ The Reiki hand positions
- ✿ Giving a complete Reiki treatment
- ✿ Using Reiki for specific conditions
- ✿ The Reiki II symbols and how to use them
- ✿ Using Reiki to heal unwanted habits
- ✿ Distant healing
- ✿ Japanese Reiki Techniques
- ✿ Hayashi Healing Guide

The class is a combination of lecture, discussion and experience. Practice time includes giving and receiving a complete Reiki treatment using all the hand positions, practicing self treatment, scanning others, beaming, using the Second Degree symbols and sending Reiki to others at a distance.

While practice takes place during the class, it is expected that you will set aside additional time to practice after the class is over. Please commit to this additional time which should be one evening a week for several weeks or its equivalent, to practice Reiki with one or more people from your Reiki class or with members of your family or friends. This additional practice is necessary to gain the experience and confidence you need to fully utilize Reiki training.

After completing one of our Reiki I &11 or ART/Master classes, nurses and massage therapists are eligible to receive contact hours for Continuing Education.

Cost $350.00 (may vary outside USA)

Advanced Reiki Training

This is a one day intensive class. It includes:

- ✿ The Usui Master attunement which increases the strength of your Reiki energy.
- ✿ The Usui Master symbol which increases the effectiveness of the Reiki II symbols and can be used for healing.
- ✿ Reiki meditation that strengthens the mind and expands the consciousness.
- ✿ Advanced techniques for using Reiki to solve problems and achieve goals.
- ✿ Using Reiki to protect yourself and others.
- ✿ The use of crystals and stones with Reiki.

- ✿ How to make a Reiki grid that will continue to send Reiki to yourself and others after it is charged.
- ✿ Reiki aura clearing that allows you to remove negative psychic energy from yourself and others and send it to the light.
- ✿ An exercise for those planning to take Reiki III/Master training.

Cost $275.00 (may vary outside USA)

A 19 page class manual is included. Note: You must take ART if you want to take Reiki Master. This class is often taught with Reiki III as a three day intensive.

Reiki Master Training

This is a two day intensive class. It includes:

☼ The complete Reiki Master Usui/ Holy Fire Master ignitions.

☼ Instruction on how to do all Reiki attunements including the Master ignitions.

☼ The Healing attunement as described on page 33.

☼ The Usui/Holy Fire system of attunements/ignitions used by the Center as well as the Usui system.

☼ One additional Holy Fire symbol for a total of five.

☼ Lots of practice time doing attunements.

☼ How to give yourself attunements and ignitions.

☼ How to send healing attunements to others at a distance.

☼ The values and spiritual orientation of a true Reiki Master.

Instruction is given on the Usui/Holy Fire system of attunements/ignitions as well as the Usui system and several variations. Over half the class time is used for practice so students become confident in administering Reiki attunements/ignitions. Students practice giving attunements on each other so that each student receives many attunements. The Healing attunement is given and received by all students. This class is a powerful healing experience. A 160 page combined ART/ Master manual is included that gives detailed steps for giving all the attunements. While the content of the class enables anyone to pass on the ability to do Reiki and to teach if one chooses, many take the class for their own use or to use with family and friends.

Cost $600.00 (may vary outside USA)

Advanced Reiki Training and Reiki Master are often taught together in one 3 day class.

Holy Fire Karuna Reiki® Training

This is an advanced class and is taught only to Reiki Masters. Karuna is a Sanskrit word that means compassionate action. This healing system was developed by William Lee Rand. It has been thoroughly tested and found to be very effective. In fact, most Reiki masters find it to be more powerful than Usui Reiki and is the next step after Reiki Master training. It contains two levels, eight practitioner symbols and one master symbol. Each symbol has a specific purpose and effect.

A description of the four Karuna I symbols is given here: The first symbol prepares the client to receive deep healing and is also useful with past life issues. The second symbol heals deeply seated issues including unconscious patterns, child and sexual abuse, shadow self issues and can release the cause of psychic and psychological attack. It also works with karmic issues on a cellular level. The third symbol fills the client with love and can be used to heal relationships, stop bad habits and create good ones, heal addictions and develop compassion. The fourth symbol grounds the client by opening the lower chakras and strengthening ones connection to the Earth. It also clears the mind, creates determination and helps manifest goals. It can be used at the end of a session to integrate and complete the healing process.

The Karuna II symbols are of a higher vibration and more powerful than those of Karuna I. They help connect directly with the Higher Self and work on a deeper level. While they have specific purposes explained in class, the experience of their energy allows intuitive guidance in their use. Both levels are taught during a three day weekend class. Upon completing the training, you will be able to practice, initiate and teach both levels of Holy Fire Karuna Reiki®. A 58 page manual and certificate is included.

Cost $875.00 (may vary outside USA)

Preparing for a Reiki Attunement

A Reiki attunement is a process of empowerment that opens your crown, heart and palm chakras and connects you to the unlimited source of Reiki energy. During the attunement, and for a time after, changes will be made by the attunement energy to enable you to channel Reiki. These changes take place metaphysically in the chakras and aura and also in the physical body. An emotional as well as a physical toxic release can take place as part of this clearing process.

In order to improve the results you receive during the attunement, a process of purification is recommended. This will allow the attunement energies to work more efficiently and create greater benefits for you. The following steps are optional. Follow them if you feel guided to do so.

1. Refrain from eating meat or fowl for three days prior to the attunement. These foods often contain drugs in the form of penicillin and female hormones, and toxins in the form of pesticides and heavy metals, that make your system sluggish and throw it out of balance.

2. Consider a water or juice fast for one to three days especially if you already are a vegetarian or have experience with fasting.

3. Minimize your use of coffee and caffeine drinks or stop completely. They create imbalances in the nervous and endocrine systems. Use no caffeine drinks on class days.

4. Use no alcohol for at least three days prior to the attunement.

5. Minimize or stop using sweets. Eat no chocolate.

6. If you smoke, cut back, and smoke as little as possible on the day of the attunement.

7. Meditate for half an hour each day for at least a week using a style you know or simply spend this time in silence.

8. Reduce or eliminate time watching TV, listening to the radio, and reading newspapers.

9. Go for quiet walks, spend time with nature, and get moderate exercise.

10. Give more attention to the subtle impressions and sensations within and around you; contemplate their meaning.

11. Release all anger, fear, jealousy, hate, worry, etc. up to the light. Create a sacred space within and around you.

While these steps are optional, they will improve your health. They will also help you have a more meaningful experience during class by helping you open to the more subtle and refined levels of Reiki energy.

Class Schedule

Reiki classes are taught under Center auspices all over the U.S. as well as in other countries. If you are interested in attending a class, please call us or check the schedule on www.reiki.org. If you would like to sponsor a class in your area please contact the Center.

ICRT Reiki Membership Association

A professional Reiki Membership Association (RMA) was started in 2010. Its purpose is to provide professional recognition for members at the same time we make it possible for those seeking Reiki sessions and classes to find qualified practitioners and teachers. It features a code of ethics and standards of practice. In addition members must be Reiki masters and agree to use the ICRT manuals in their classes.

Benefits of the RMA

RMA members enjoy an effective method of advertising their Reiki practices. The membership list is advertised on the www.reiki.org home page that gets over 3000 visits a day. This generates over 4-500 visits to our member list by those seeking Reiki practitioners and teachers, thus creating referrals for our members. Members are also provided with a brochure to promote their Reiki businesses. This is a professionally produced brochure that clearly explains what Reiki is, how it works, what a session is like, and also provides scientific validation for its therapeutic value. The members contact information is automatically placed on the brochure by the computer program and are downloadable from our web site so members can obtain them instantly and print them on their home printer. An additional benefit is a secure online database that can be used to keep track of your classes and students as well as the ability to create Reiki class certificates online and download them to your printer. As soon as you join, you'll be provided with an ICRT Reiki Membership Association certificate that you'll be able to display on the wall of your Reiki room or show to prospective clients or students. As a member, you'll have exclusive access to our Group Page where you'll be able to post notices and share information with other members. Available to members is a special Reiki insurance policy. One policy covers Reiki and over 300 other modalities, including most forms of massage, body work and energy therapy. A special member price for the insurance is available. There are many other member benefits. To learn more or to join, please go to www.reikimembership.com. (Also see pages 174-175.)

Reiki Web Site

We have a 500+ page Internet Web Site. It provides access to over 300 articles covering every aspect of Reiki practice, Reiki stories, the Global Healing Network, a listing of our classes world-wide and much more.

Web site address **http://www.reiki.org**
E-mail **Center@reiki.org**

**The International Center
for Reiki Training
Phone (800) 332-8112, (248) 948-8112
Fax (248) 948-9534**

Anatomy *for* Reiki

ILLUSTRATIONS BY TOM BOWMAN

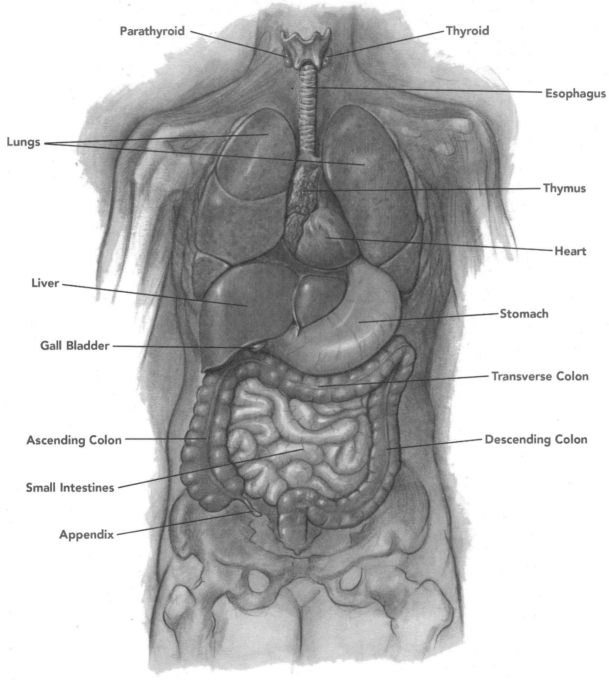

Parathyroid

Thyroid

Esophagus

Lungs

Thymus

Heart

Liver

Stomach

Gall Bladder

Transverse Colon

Ascending Colon

Descending Colon

Small Intestines

Appendix

Front View

While an extensive understanding of anatomy is not necessary for Reiki practitioners, there are times when a basic knowledge of the major organs of the body is helpful, and even necessary. These include when the client has a condition or illness involving a specific organ(s) that needs treatment or when working in a clinic or hospital where communication with medical personnel about a client's condition is necessary.

Adrenals: Part of the endocrine system, the adrenals secrete hormones that regulate various functions in the body, one of which is the flight or fight response.

Appendix: The appendix is located at the beginning of the colon on the lower right side of the abdominal cavity. It is medically said to have no function.

Colon: Consisting of the ascending, transverse and descending sections, this tube-like organ is also called the large intestine and joins the small intestine on the lower right side of the abdominal cavity. The final processes of digestion take place in the colon with the absorption of water from fecal matter.

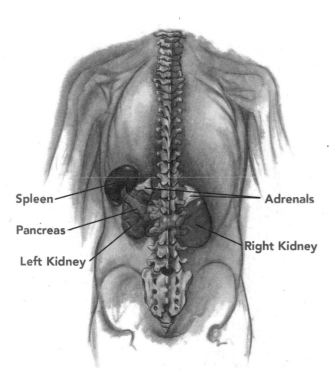

Spleen
Pancreas
Left Kidney
Adrenals
Right Kidney

Back View

Esophagus: The esopagus is the portion of the digestive tube that moves food from the mouth to the stomach.

Gallbladder: Connected to the liver, the gallbladder stores and secretes bile, which aids digestion of fats.

Heart: This is the muscular organ that pumps blood to all parts of the body. The rhythmic beating of the heart is a ceaseless activity, lasting from before birth to the end of life.

Kidneys: The purpose of the kidneys is to separate urea, mineral salts, toxins and other waste products from the blood, and to conserve water, salts and electrolytes.

Liver: The liver is the largest glandular organ of the body and has many functions including filtering debris and bacteria from the blood, converting excess carbohydrates and protein into fats and producing blood-clotting factors and vitamins A, D, K and B12. It also produces bile, which is used to prepare fats for digestion.

Lungs: The lungs are elastic organs used for breathing; they oxygenate the blood.

Pancreas: The pancreas is a glandular organ that secretes digestive enzymes and hormones. It also produces insulin, which lowers the blood-sugar level and increases the amount of glycogen (stored carbohydrate) in the liver.

Parathyroid: These four small glands are often embedded in the thyroid gland and govern calcium and phosphorus metabolism.

Small Intestine: Located between the stomach and colon, the small intestine digests and absorbs nutrients from food. This process is aided by secretions from the liver and pancreas.

Spleen: The spleen acts as a filter against foreign organisms that infect the bloodstream, and also filters out old red blood cells from the bloodstream and decomposes them.

Stomach: The stomach is the part of the digestive tract between the esophagus and the small intestine.

Thymus: The thymus gland helps in the development and functioning of the immune system.

Thyroid: Part of the endocrine system, the thyroid gland secretes hormones necessary for growth and metabolism.

Reiki Client Information Form

Name: (Please Print) _____

Phone (home): _____ Cell phone or evening: _____

Address: _____

City, State, Zip: _____

Email (optional): _____

Emergency Contact: _____

Current Medications and dosage: _____

_____

_____

Are you currently under the care of a physician? ___ Yes ___ No

If yes, physician's name: _____

How did you hear about us? _____

_____

Have you ever had a Reiki session before? ___Yes ___No

If yes, when was your last session? _____

Number of previous sessions _____

Do you have a particular area of concern? _____

_____

_____

Are you sensitive to perfumes or fragrances? _____

Are you sensitive to touch? _____

I understand that Reiki is a simple, gentle, hands-on energy technique that is used for stress reduction and relaxation. I understand that Reiki practitioners do not diagnose conditions nor do they prescribe or perform medical treatment, prescribe substances, nor interfere with the treatment of a licensed medical professional. I understand that Reiki does not take the place of medical care. It is recommended that I see a licensed physician or licensed health care professional for any physical or psychological aliment I may have. I understand that Reiki can complement any medical or psychological care I may be receiving. I also understand that the body has the ability to heal itself and to do so, complete relaxation is often beneficial. I acknowledge that long term imbalances in the body sometimes require multiple sessions in order to facilitate the level of relaxation needed by the body to heal itself.

Signed: _____ Date: _____

Privacy Notice:

No information about any client will be discussed or shared with any third party without written consent of the client or parent/guardian if the client is under 18.

148

Reiki Documentation Form

Client Name: _____ Date: _____

Reason for Session
___ Relaxation and Stress Reduction
___ Specific Issue:

    Physical _____

    _____

    Emotional _____

    _____

    Mental/Spiritual _____

    _____

Changes since last session: _____
_____
_____

Observation / Scan before Reiki Session: _____
_____
_____

Observation / Scan after Reiki Session: _____
_____
_____
_____

Post Session Notes: _____
_____
_____
_____
_____
_____
_____

Length / Type of Session: _____
Follow up Planned: _____
_____
_____

Practitioner Name: _____

The Beaming Reiki Masters

This picture was taken at a Reiki III Master class in Toledo, Ohio. The class members used the distant symbol and projected the Reiki power symbol into the camera, intending that all who see the resultant picture would receive Reiki energy. Clairvoyant observation indicates that Reiki energy comes directly from the Reiki source and does not pass through those in the picture. Place it in front of you or carry it with you. It can be used by itself or in conjunction with hands on Reiki or other healing or meditation techniques. Feel free to experiment with it and make copies of this page to give to friends.

Takata's Masters

Mrs. Takata initiated twenty-two Reiki Masters between 1970 and her transition in 1980. Below is a list of the Reiki Masters she initiated. This is the list she gave to her sister before she passed through transition.

George Araki	Phyllis Lei Furumoto
Barbara McCullough	Dorothy Baba (deceased)
Beth Gray (deceased)	Mary McFadyen
Ursula Baylow (deceased)	John Gray (deceased)
Paul Mitchell	Rick Bockner
Iris Ishikura (deceased)	Bethel Phaigh (deceased)
Fran Brown (deceased)	Harry Kuboi
Barbara Weber Ray	Patricia Ewing
Ethel Lombardi	Shinobu Saito
Wanja Twan	Takata's Sister
Virginia Samdahl (deceased)	Barbara Brown

Reading List

Arnold, L. and S. Nevius. *The Reiki Handbook*. Harrisburg, PA: PSI Press, 1982.

Baginski, B. and S. Sharamon. *Reiki: Universal Life Energy*. Mendocino, CA: Life Rhythm Pub., 1985.

Brennan, B. *Hands of Light*. New York: Bantam Books, 1988.

Brown, F. *Living Reiki: Takata's Teachings*. Life Rhythm, 1992.

Doi, H. *Iyashino Gendai Reiki-ho*. Coquitlam, B.C., Canada: Fraser Journal Publishing, 2000.

Gerber, R. *Vibrational Medicine*. Santa Fe, NM: Bear & Co., 1988.

Gleisner, E. *Reiki In Everyday Living*. White Feather Press, 1992.

Haberly, H. *Reiki: Hawayo Takata's Story*. Garrett Park, MD: Archedigm Pub., 1990.

Heinz, S. *Healing Magnetism*. Your Beach, Maine: Samuel Weiser, Inc., 1987.

Hochhuth, K. *Practical Guide to Reiki: an Ancient Healing Art*, Victoria, Australia: Gemcrafters Books, 1993.

Horan, P. *Empowerment through Reiki*. Wilmot, WI: Lotus Light Pub., 1990.

Jarrel, D. *Reiki Plus First Degree*. Edenton, NC: Reiki Plus Institute, 1984.

Jarrel, D. *Reiki Plus Professional Practitioners Manual for Second Degree*. Edenton, NC: Reiki Plus Institute, 1992.

Krieger, D. *The Therapeutic Touch*. New York: Prentice Hall Press, 1986.

Kunz, D. *Spiritual Aspects of the Healing Arts*. Wheaton, IL: The Theosophical Publishing House. Kushi, M. and O. Oredson. *Macrobiotic Palm Healing*. New York: Japan Pub., Inc., 1988.

Lubeck, W. *The Complete Reiki Handbook*. Twin Lakes, WI: Lotus Light Publications, 1994.

Lugenbeel, B. *Virginia Samdahl: Reiki Master Healer*. Norfolk, VA: Gunwald and Radcliff Pub., 1984.

Mitchell, P. *The Blue Book*. Cataldo, ID: The Reiki Alliance, 1985.

Petter, F. *The Original Reiki Handbook of Dr. Mikao Usui*. Twin Lakes, WI: Lotus Light Pub. 1999.

Petter, F. *Reiki Fire*. Twin Lakes, WI: Lotus Light Pub., 1997.

Petter, F. *Reiki, The Legacy of Dr. Usui*. Twin Lakes, WI: Lotus Light Pub. 1998.

Petter, F., T. Yamaguchi, C. Hayashi. *The Hayashi Reiki Manual*. Twin Lakes, WI: Lotus Light Pub., 2002.

Rand, W. *Reiki For A New Millennium*. Southfield, MI: Vision Pub., 1998.

Rand, W, F. Petter, W. Lubeck. *The Spirit of Reiki*. Twin Lakes, WI: Lotus Light Pub., 2000.

Ray, B. *The Reiki Factor*. St. Petersburg, FL: Radiance Associates, 1983.

Stewart, J.C. *The Reiki Touch*. Houston, TX: The Reiki Touch, Inc., 1989.

Yamaguchi, T. *Light on the Origins of Reiki*. Twin Lakes, WI: Lotus Press, 2007.

Notes

Notes

Notes

Appendix D

How Hawayo Takata
Practiced and Taught Reiki

How Hawayo Takata Practiced and Taught Reiki

BY MARIANNE STREICH

Mrs. Takata at the Baylow home, June 11, 1979. (Photo taken by G. Baylow.)

All Western Reiki practitioners have a lineage going back through Mrs. Takata. It was she who brought Reiki to the West. Without her, it is unlikely that anyone outside Japan would even recognize the word "Reiki" today, much less know the wonderful gift of its healing power.

Takata practiced and taught Reiki for more than forty years. She was a powerful healer, an engaging teacher, and a successful businesswoman. She facilitated amazing healings, attuned countless men, women, and children to Reiki, and managed a number of business enterprises. What she did not do was leave comprehensive records about her work.

Unlike Usui sensei and Hayashi sensei, Takata did not provide her students with a manual or printed materials.[1] She did not allow the taking of notes during her classes; her teaching was in the oral tradition, and she expected her students to store her words in memory. Likewise, papers on which students practiced drawing the Reiki symbols were destroyed at the end of each class.[2] Takata had no prepared text and so each of her classes was somewhat different.[3] She left no known written records of her work or philosophy.

In part because of her oral system of teaching, many rumors and myths have developed about her over the years, and it can be challenging to reconstruct accurate information. We must rely on the memories and writings of the twenty-two Masters (see list page 164) she trained and on her Level I and II students to reconstruct her methods of practicing and teaching. This I have attempted to do, accessing as many sources and materials as possible.

Takata's Training

In her book, *Living Reiki*,[4] Fran Brown describes Takata's training as Takata explained it to her. According to Brown, Takata spent a year of internship at Dr. Hayashi's clinic in Tokyo, beginning in 1935. She was initiated into the First Degree of Reiki over four days. On the first day, students were taught basic hand positions for treating above the neck and the conditions and diseases common to those areas. On day two, they were taught hand positions and treatment of conditions of the front of the body and on day three, the back. Day four was devoted to treatment of acute cases and accidents and to discussion of the spiritual aspects of Reiki and the Five Ideals. Each student was given a copy of Hayashi's healing guide, which gave a list of diseases and the hand positions that were to be used in the treatment of each condition. He also emphasized that there is always a cause and an effect; eliminate the cause and there will be no effect.

After this training, Hayashi's students spent mornings in his clinic working in pairs to treat patients and afternoons making house calls, giving treatments that typically lasted an hour to an hour and a half each. At the end of her year of internship, she was given an examination and allowed to progress to the Second Degree or *Oku Den*.[5] After this more training was offered. A May 1936 entry in Takata's diary reads:

> What was more than pleasing was that Mr. Hayashi has granted to bestow upon me the secret of *Shinpe Den*, *Kokiyu-ho* and the *Leiji-ho* the utmost secret in the Energy Science. Know [sic] one can imagine my happiness to think that I have the honor and respect to be trusted with this gift a gift of a life time and I promised within me to do my utmost in regard to this beautiful and wonderful teaching that I just received—I fully promise to do what is right thru sincereness [sic] and to do my utmost in kindness and shall regard and respect the teaching and it's teacher with utmost reverence and respect.[6]

The sign for Takata's office was discovered in the basement of her clinic by Reiki Master Duff Cady in 1995. The clinic was located at 2070 Kilauea Ave. in Hilo, Hawaii. The word "Reiki" is visible behind the lettering. The change from Reiki to "Short Wave Treatments" was probably in response to anti-Japanese sentiment after the bombing of Pearl Harbor in December of 1941. The building currently houses the Kline Chiropractic Clinic. Dr. Kline, an Aikido instructor and healer, has set up a small shrine on the upper floor to honor Hawayo Takata.

In the summer of 1937[7] Takata returned to Kauai. A few weeks later Hayashi sensei came to visit her. He stayed for six months, giving classes and treatments with Takata briefly on Kauai, then in Honolulu. Hayashi sensei issued her a Master certificate on February 21, 1938 (see photo page 165). To avoid licensing issues, the following year Takata studied at the National College of Drugless Physicians in Chicago and also received a license to practice massage in Honolulu. (Brown, 68) In October of 1939 she moved her office to Hilo on the big island where she remained for the next ten years. (Brown, 71)

---

[1] Dr. Hayashi's manual is translated and reprinted in *Reiki, The Healing Touch, First and Second Degree Manual* by William Lee Rand (Michigan: Vision Publications, 2000). A partial translation of Dr. Usui's manual is available in *The Original Reiki Handbook of Dr. Mikao Usui: The Traditional Usui Reiki Ryoho Treatment Positions and Numerous Reiki Techniques for Health and Well-Being* by Mikao Usui, Frank Arjava Petter (Wisconsin: Lotus Press, 2000).

[2] Amy Z. Rowland, in "A Tribute to Traditional Reiki Master, Rev. Beth Gray," *Reiki News Magazine* (Spring 2003), 10, states: "She [Beth Gray, one of the twenty-two Masters that Takata trained] had promised Takata that she would collect all drawings of the symbols at the close of each Level II class, and afterwards, burn them. And this she did."

[3] Dr. Paul V. Johnson, president Spiritual Advisory Council, in a letter to William Lee Rand dated April 19, 1994 states: "I sat in on a number [of her classes] and all were somewhat different as she had no prepared text."

(Johnson was a Level I and II student of Takata's. He and his wife hosted Takata in their home for several of these classes during 1975-1976.)

[4] Fran Brown, *Living Reiki, Takata's Teachings* (California: LifeRhythm, 1992), 29-30.

[5] I have found no information regarding the content of her *Oku Den*, or Second Degree training with Dr. Hayashi.

[6] Hawayo Takata, unpublished diary. *Shinpe Den* is the master level, *Kokiyu-ho* is the dry bathing technique and *Leiji-ho* is the intuitive method of finding where to place one's hands.

[7] Helen Joyce Haberly, *Reiki: Hawayo Takata's Story* (Maryland: Archedigm Publications, 2000 Memorial Edition), 33. Fran Brown gives 1936 as the year of Takata's return to Kauai; however, since Haberly's text was authorized by Takata and much of it was written during Takata's lifetime, 1937 seems the more likely date. In addition, the date of Takata's Master certificate also supports the later date.

This is an ad for Takata's Hilo practice, which appeared in the local *Tribune Herald*, March 3, 1941, prior to the attack on Pearl Harbor.

Takata's Practice

Takata's Reiki treatment consisted of what she called a "foundation treatment" followed by a search for the cause of the condition and additional Reiki applied in those specific areas related to the cause. She advocated repeated treatments, daily if possible, for chronic conditions. And she welcomed what she called "healing reactions" as a sign that the body was beginning to heal itself.

According to Takata-trained Master John Harvey Gray,[8] Takata combined many of the hand positions taught by Dr. Hayashi to create her "foundation treatment," which she used as a standard procedure for each client. In contrast, Hayashi employed a specific combination of positions to treat specific conditions. In his clinic, two practitioners worked together to give a treatment, whereas Takata worked alone, giving treatments sitting on the floor in a cross-legged fashion. (Gray, 97)

Her foundation treatment focused on the torso and the head. According to Gray, there were four basic hand positions for the torso and three for the head. (Gray, 93). There were none over the heart or on the back, although she added optional positions over the heart, the back, and on the back of the head, depending on the nature of the client's problem. The first hand

Mrs. Takata by Ursula Baylow's garden near Skaha Lake, Penticton, BC, June, 1979. (Photo taken by G. Baylow.)

position in a foundation treatment covered the area of the stomach, pancreas, and spleen.[9] The second position covered the liver and gall bladder, a third covered the transverse colon and the small intestine, and the fourth placement covered the reproductive system, ascending and descending colon, and bladder (see photos page 160). Brown reports that Takata admonished her students to spend half of the treatment time on the front torso, as it is the "main factory" of the body, processing the fuel that the body takes in (Brown 29).

After treating the torso, Takata then moved to the head, using three positions, and sometimes adding a fourth on the back of the head. The first position covered the eyes; with the second, hands were placed on either side of the head, and in the third, hands were placed on the neck. This was a complete foundation treatment. On many occasions, according to Gray, Takata remarked that she had simplified the system (Gray, 94).

Gray reports that Takata's foundation treatment began with the torso (Gray, 93), although other practitioners recall her starting with the head. Helen Haberly reports that Takata sometimes started a treatment with the head, at other times with the abdomen. At times she told her students that it didn't matter as long as the complete treatment was given. (Haberly, 50) In some instances she indicated that the nature of the condition determines where the treatment should start. "The complete treatment is given, but in these cases [arthritis and rheumatism] we start with the abdomen." (Haberly, 73) And again, "For all types, [of cancer] the same procedure is used: the complete treatment is given. Start from the head, then treat all of the glands on the front of the body. Turn the patient over and complete the back. Last of all, go to the affected area." (Haberly, 99)

One of Takata's guiding principles, which she emphasized repeatedly, was to treat both cause and effect. "If you treat only the afflicted area of the body, you may alleviate symptoms temporarily but permanent healing will not take place unless you treat the cause." (Gray, 80) Takata's training and experience had taught her that the cause of a condition is often centered, not in the affected area of the body, but elsewhere. She tells of treating a young woman who had become blind around the age of thirteen for no apparent reason. She was brought to Takata three years later after attempts to discover the cause of her condition through traditional medicine had failed. Had Takata only treated the girl's eyes, she would not have discovered that the cause of the condition was actually in the ovaries. Takata

---

[8] John Harvey Gray and Lourdes Gray with Steven McFadden and Elisabeth Clark, *Hand to Hand, The Longest-Practicing Reiki Master Tells His Story* (Gray, 2002).

[9] Although Gray indicates on page 93 that the first position is over the liver, a later reference on page 98 and photo on page 115 make it clear that the first position is over the stomach, pancreas and spleen. Haberly's text also indicates that the first position is over the stomach.

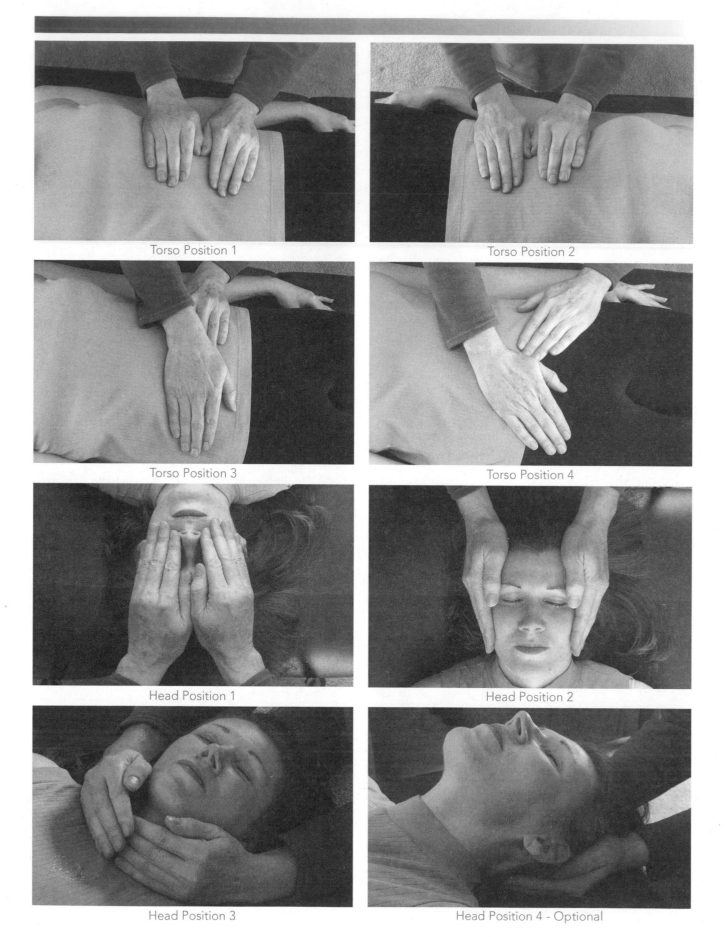

Torso Position 1

Torso Position 2

Torso Position 3

Torso Position 4

Head Position 1

Head Position 2

Head Position 3

Head Position 4 - Optional

160

Summer 1979, at Penticton BC, with Ursula Baylow, when she completed her training as Reiki Master. (photo taken by G. Baylow)

treated her daily for 28 days, giving a full treatment and additional energy to the ovaries and eyes. On the 28th day, she could see again. (Gray, 81)

To locate the cause, Takata used her intuition. This was likely a simplified version of *Leiji-ho* (also called *Reiji-ho*), a technique taught to her by Hayashi.[10] She also used the sensitivity in her hands to locate the cause by noticing a stronger or different vibration when her hands were over the part of the body where the cause of a condition was centered. This was probably a simplified version of Byosen scanning. She told her students, "Reiki will guide you. Let the Reiki hands find it. They will know what to do." (Haberly, 58)

At times Takata started a treatment in the area where the cause was located. Haberly relates that a man came to Takata with the complaint that he suffered headaches every evening. Takata began treating his abdomen in the area of his gall bladder. When he protested that he had a headache, not a stomachache, she explained that she felt "much vibration in my hands" when she reached the area of his gall bladder and felt that the cause of his discomfort was there. She followed this by working on his head and his back, giving a full treatment. The client reported that by the time she came to his head, the pain was gone. (Haberly, 78) For breast cancer or any condition involving the breasts, Takata advocated special emphasis on the ovaries, uterus (torso position 4) and thyroid, (head position 3) as she found that the cause of the condition was often located in these areas. (Haberly, 99-100)

"Takata always encouraged complete and frequent Reiki treatments for long-lasting chronic problems, daily, if possible. She emphasized that if a health problem or illness has been around for three weeks or more, the whole body is involved in the healing process and therefore a full treatment is indicated." (Gray, 81) In the recounting of her stories, Takata frequently mentions giving treatments daily, sometimes several times a day, over lengthy periods of time. In a case of shingles, for instance, she reports giving the client treatment daily for two months, by which time the pain had disappeared. The client took Reiki and

continued to treat herself daily afterwards. (Haberly, 95) In another case, Takata treated a young woman with epilepsy. "We began treatments in October and by the Spring I said she did not have to come to me any more, for the family could treat her at home. She continued to improve, and in this way she was entirely cured of epilepsy." (Haberly, 69-70)

Haberly quotes Takata as saying, "Except for shock or accident, use the full treatment, and this is the same for all things. Don't try to take only the parts. The body is a complete unit, so whenever possible, treat it completely. Start with the abdomen or the head—it doesn't matter—then proceed with the whole treatment. It is the same for all, whether physical or mental. There is no difference in the treatment." (Haberly, 59)

When treating someone who had experienced trauma, Takata would "release shock from the adrenal glands" by placing the hands over the adrenal glands and giving Reiki until the flow of energy diminished. Gray quotes Takata as saying, "There will not be complete healing after an injury if you don't release the shock from the adrenals." (Gray, 172)

At the end of a treatment, Takata used a technique that involved running the fingers on either side of the spine and manipulating tissue from the neck to coccyx to improve blood circulation. (Gray, 94) (This technique is sometimes referred to as "The Reiki Finish" or "Nerve Stroke.") Since performing this technique requires a massage license in many jurisdictions, Gray and other practitioners have devised alternate techniques that accomplish the same goal without manipulation of tissue. One method is to sweep the hands through the energy field from head to foot several times.

To ensure that her clients received treatment on a regular basis, Takata often attuned members of their families, and in at least one instance, their neighbors. Helen Haberly relates a story about a young woman who had advanced tuberculosis. Takata gave her treatments every day for a week and then gave classes to her mother and their neighbors so that she could have many people treating her. According to Takata, she completely recovered within six months. (Haberly, 82)

After a treatment, especially one for a chronic condition, Takata expected the client to experience a "healing reaction." This was a release of toxins by the body and could take the form of gastrointestinal upset, flu-like symptoms, headache, or in some instances an intensification of the condition itself. (Haberly, 69) Takata welcomed healing reactions because "the reaction shows whether the healing is moving forward." (Brown, 92) According to Haberly, Takata taught that chronic conditions requiring long-term treatment are more likely to be accompanied by reactions that release toxins. If injuries are quickly treated they are not as likely to produce reactions. (Haberly, 55)

Although most of Takata's stories focus on the treatment of illness, she also emphasized the importance of Reiki to ensure health and well-being. For instance, regarding Reiki and pregnancy, she is quoted as saying, "The best plan is to start Reiki before becoming pregnant, and then have treatments to strengthen her during the pregnancy; and if any symptoms then appear, Reiki could be applied immediately." (Haberly, 67)

Whatever the condition, Takata's philosophy was to "give a good treatment and release it to God. Leave it to God how healing will come about." (Brown, 95)

How Takata Taught

Takata taught in Hawaii for a number of years before starting to teach classes on the mainland in the 1970's. The first mainland class she taught that included students of non-Japanese origin was taught on Orcas Island off the coast of Washington state in 1973. (Gray, 71) She often held classes in private homes, teaching a number of classes from 1974-1977 in Redmond, CA at the home of Beth and John Harvey Gray. Before her death in 1980, she had traveled the world teaching countless students and training twenty-two Masters.

Takata's Reiki I classes were typically taught over the course of three or four evenings in sessions that typically lasted two hours but could, at times, go on for up to four hours, according to Brown. (Brown, 94) She did not work from a prepared text, so the content, as well as the length of the classes, varied. She began with an explanation of Universal energy, "Here is the great space which surrounds us—the Universe. There is endless and enormous energy. It is universal…its ultimate source is the Creator…it can stem from the sun, or moon or stars…. It is a limitless force. It is the source of energy that makes the plants grow…the birds fly. When a human being has pain, problems, he or she can draw from it. It is an ethereal source, a wave length of great power which can revitalize, restore harmony."[11]

She told the story of Usui sensei in installments over the course of the class, a segment prior to each of four attunements. She demonstrated and explained hand positions. She was very precise about the placement of the hands. Master Wanja Twan remembers "Mrs. Takata's crisp teachings and precise hand positions, a perfect technician…"[12] A student of Master Beth Gray reports that Beth Gray's students were taught to keep their hands in the same position through an entire cycle of energy [until the practitioner begins to feel energy ebb in the hands] and were told that was Takata's teaching.[13]

During her classes, Takata told numerous stories about her forty-plus years of experience with the treatment of various conditions from tuberculosis to blindness to arthritis to headache. A natural storyteller with a keen sense of humor, her tales were entertaining as well as instructive. She talked about the Five Reiki Ideals. She used repetition to make sure that each of her students understood, as she did not allow the taking of notes or taping of classes.[14] (She did allow John Gray to tape some of the stories she told during her classes, and one of those tapes is available.)[15]

Reiki Juice

Takata recommended a diet of vegetables, fruits, whole grains, fish and chicken. She also had a home remedy, a drink which she drank and recommended to her clients and students. (Some of her students called it the Takata Cocktail.) She said it purifies the blood and energizes the whole body. Helen Haberly mentions it in, *Reiki: Hawayo Takata's Story*, but does not give an actual recipe. Being a juicer, I was curious and experimented with the ingredients. Here's what I came up with:

All ingredients should be organic, but if not, then make sure you wash them with a vegetable wash to remove pesticidial residues and chemical sprays (available in most health food stores).

1	beet about 2 inches in diameter. You can also include some of the greens.
1	tablespoon watercress or about 10 small leaves.
2	stalks of celery
1	medium carrot
2	cups purified or spring water.
3-5	minutes Reiki

Chop up all ingredients and place in a high speed blender such as a Vita Mix. Before blending, place your hands on the blender container and give Reiki to the ingredients for several minutes. Start the blender and continue giving Reiki until the mixture is liquefied.

In addition to being a blood purifier, this concoction is a powerful detoxifier, especially for the liver, gallbladder and lungs. The affects of this drink are very beneficial, but caution should be exercised when first starting to consume it because it is such a powerful detoxifier.

Drink only about half the juice at first, placing the remainder in the refrigerator. Wait an hour or more before drinking more to discover how your body will respond to it. Once you've determined the amount that is right for you, it's important that you drink Reiki Juice every day as its beneficial effects take place over time. It has a really fresh wholesome flavor but a little on the tart side. Drinking it gives you increased mental clarity, a feeling of lightness, energy and vitality that will only increase as your body detoxifies.

—*William Lee Rand*

---

[10] Takata's diary, unpublished.

[11] Fran Brown, "Mrs. Takata Opens Minds to Reiki," San Mateo, *The Times*, May 17, 1975.

[12] Wanja Twan, Web posting, www.morningstarproductions.ca/page2.htm

[13] Amy Z. Rowland, "A Tribute to Traditional Reiki Master, Rev. Beth Gray" *Reiki News Magazine* (Spring 2003), 10.

[14] The information in this paragraph is cited in numerous sources, including, John Harvey Gray, Fran Brown, Amy Z. Rowland (student of Beth Gray), Sarah Baylow, daughter of Ursula Baylow, Anneli Twan, daughter of Wanja Twan, and others who took Level I and II from Takata.

[15] "Takata Speaks, Volume I Reiki Stories," Selections and Introductions by John Harvey Gray, available through Gray's Web site: www.mv.com/ipusers/reiki/

Classes were focused and intense. Anneli Twan (daughter of Master Wanja Twan) remembers Takata as "an exceedingly efficient teacher....when that little Japanese fireball said 'jump' everyone jumped."[16] Robert Shingledecker, a student who hosted Takata's classes in his home, recalls, "Mrs. Takata took her Reiki very seriously and could be a taskmaster and disciplinarian, but she was also sweet, even motherly to us and had a heart bigger than she was."[17]

Shingledecker remembers that she talked about different illnesses and how to treat them and emphasized certain "no no's" such as "never lay hands on the spine—always come in from an angle[18] and never remove your hands from the patient—even when rolling him/her over."[19] He relates that Takata told him privately that a Reiki practitioner should remove all jewelry prior to giving a Reiki session because it can get very hot. (Shingledecker, Web posting)

Takata advocated to her students and clients a diet of vegetables, fruits, whole grains, fish and chicken. Helen Haberly mentions a recipe for a Reiki Juice home remedy that Takata concocted, which consisted of watercress, beets, carrots, and celery blended together. Takata claimed that it was a blood builder that energized the entire body. (Haberly, 48) Shingledecker refers to this as the "Takata Cocktail," of which he said, "...it looked gorgeous...but tasted horrible!" He recalled that it had a number of ingredients, including beet greens, and said that Takata insisted that he drink it every day when she was holding classes in his home. (Shingledecker, Web posting) An avid juicer, William Rand has experimented with the ingredients and devised a recipe. (See page 164.)

Takata stressed to her students the importance of treating themselves. "'You are Number One!' she would say, 'Then if you have time, treat your family and your friends; but in Reiki Healing, you first, then other people.'" (Haberly, 56) After the Level I attunement, Takata had her students give her treatments each evening.[20] "She told us that when one practices Reiki they would have health, happiness, security and should prepare for a long life...she once told me that when you had pure Reiki flowing through you, you could not make a bad decision." (Shingledecker, Web posting)

There is less information available as to how Takata taught her Level II or "Distant Healing" classes as they were called. She taught the three symbols and how to give distant Reiki. Initially, only the dominant hand was initiated during the Level II attunement.[21] This was later changed either by Takata or some of her Masters. It is now common practice to initiate both hands.

In some instances, Takata gave two attunements during the Level II class rather than one. According to Rowland, "The attunement process using two attunements...opened up a special channel in the mind of the practitioner which facilitated an intuitive ability. This enhanced the practitioner's ability to communicate with the subconscious mind of the client to find the original cause of an illness or condition and also allowed the practitioner to communicate with the clients Higher Self."[22] This information was accessed through the use of the Mental/Emotional symbol, which Beth Gray also called "the talking symbol." (Rowland, 10) When two attunements are given, the second is a repeat of the first according to John Gray. In his experience, whether the second attunement increases a student's intuition varies depending on the student.[23]

Little mention is made of the length of the Level II classes or the specifics of what was taught, except for the learning of symbols. Several sources relate that Takata sometimes taught Level II back to back with Level I,[24] although a time period for Level II is not mentioned. She was very exacting about the teaching of the symbols and had students practice them over and over. After the class, she burned all of the practice papers, as students were to have memorized them. Takata considered the symbols sacred and admonished her students that they were not to be shown to anyone who was not already attuned to Reiki.[25]

Paul Johnson hosted classes in his Golf, Illinois home in 1975-1976. He states that the class in which he and his wife and eight others were initiated into Reiki II in 1976 lasted only two hours, with Takata commenting that the group was "exceptionally gifted" and caught on quickly. The class consisted largely of learning to draw the three symbols.[26]

Master Wanja Twan reports that she took part in five Level I classes and three Level II classes taught by Takata in rural British Columbia in the late 70's, one of which was a special

[16] Anneli Twan, from a talk quoted on Holistic Vancouver Web site: http://www.holisticvancouver.com/news/article.php?story_id=125. Twan received her first attunement in the spring of 1979 at the age of ten. She received her Master level from her mother, Wanja Twan with the help of Phyllis Furumoto (Takata's granddaughter) and taught her first class at the age of sixteen.

[17] William R. Shingledecker, 1997 Web posting: www.create.org/healingarts/takata.htm. This site is no longer active.

[18] Not touching the spine may have come from the idea that only a licensed chiropractor should touch the spine, but we know from experience that the spine can be treated without harm as long as one doesn't manipulate the vertebra.

[19] John Gray, in a telephone conversation January 30, 2007 told the

author that, to his knowledge, Takata never suggested a practitioner should keep his/her hands on the client throughout the treatment.

[20] Dr. Paul V. Johnson, letter to William Rand, April 19, 1994.

[21] Rowland mentions this, as do other practitioners.

[22] In the same article, Rowland states: "As far as I know, Takata taught only three other Reiki Masters she initiated to use the second symbol in an intuitive way, and she did not teach them identically..."

[23] John Gray, telephone conversation with the author, January 30, 2007.

[24] Wanja Twan, Paul Johnson, and Shingledecker in Web postings and letter previously cited.

[25] It is safe to say that virtually all of her students and Masters would agree on this.

[26] Paul V. Johnson in a letter to William Rand dated March 14, 1994.

class for children.[27] Twan took Level I in summer 1978, Level II in spring of 1979 and Master in October of 1979. At the time she received Master, a class was held in which she assisted, "…there were so many people gathered, Mrs. Takata at this time instructed me as if she was an army sergeant how to do the actual teachings [Level I] and the mechanics of it. Ten people indicated that they wanted their second degree at that time, so I had good practice in that as well."[28]

Length of time period between Level II and Master Level and the length of the Master Level training itself also varied. Fran Brown relates that she took Level I from Takata in 1973, Level II in 1977 and was initiated as Takata's seventh Master in January 1979.[29] Although she doesn't specify the number of sessions nor the total hours of training, she states in her book, *Living Reiki*, that she and Takata were snowbound for a week during her Master training and that she team taught with Takata as part of her training. (Brown, 94)

Bethal Phaigh's experience was quite different. She received Level II and Master initiations within a few days of each other. "Now I have to drive two hundred miles back to the Slocan [British Columbia] to get the money [for the Master training] and then back again to Lumby, [to] be initiated as a Master. All this and second degree within a few days!"[30] She continues, "I had left Hawaii that spring [1979] not knowing of Reiki. I return this winter as a Reiki Master, a very green one." (Phaigh, 132) That same winter she met up with Takata again on the Big Island, where Takata was visiting for one day only. That evening Takata re-attuned Phaigh. (Phaigh, 133)

In addition to Brown, some of the other Masters Takata trained, including Virginia Samdahl and Phyllis Furomoto, may have traveled with her as part of their training, but this seems not to have been the case for most of them.[31] John Gray has no memory of any of the other Masters serving such an apprenticeship.[32]

In her Master classes, Takata taught four attunements for Level I and one or perhaps two for Level II.[33] She gave one Master symbol. The focus of the Master training was on learning how to pass attunements. Twan quotes Takata as instructing her Master students, "Keep it [instruction] simple or people will forget." (Twan, Web posting)

Her Legacy

Mrs. Takata made her transition on December 25, 1980, just short of her eightieth birthday. Without her, it is very unlikely

Takata's Masters

	First	Second	Master
Iris Ishikuro	1967		?
Kay Yamashita			before 1976
John Harvey Gray	06/1974		10/6/1976
Virginia W. Samdahl		1975	before 10/1976
Ethel Lombardi	1976?	1976?	1976
Dorothy Baba			1977
Barbara Lincoln McCullough			1977
Harry M. Kuboi			04/1977
Fran Brown	06/1973	1977	01/15/1979
Phyllis Lei Furumoto			04/1979
Ursula Baylow	07/ 7/1976	08/25/1978	06/11/1979
Barbara Weber	08/1978	10/1978	09/1979
Barbara Brown			10/1979
Beth Gray	1973		10/1979
Bethal Phaigh	Spring 1979	10/1979	10/1979
Wanja Twan	Summer 1978	Spring 1979	10/1979
George Araki			11/1979
Paul Mitchell			11/1979
Shinobu Saito		1978	05/1980
Mary McFadyen			09/1980
Patricia Bowling			09/1980
Rick Bockner	10/10/1979	10/20/1979	10/12/1980

that Reiki would ever have reached the West. Certainly there was little communication and cultural interaction between Japan and the West in the late 1930's when she learned Reiki and brought it to Hawaii, and it is highly unlikely that Japanese practitioners would have had any thought or desire of exporting Reiki to the West in the aftermath of World War II.

The impact that Reiki has had in the world is largely due to Takata's extraordinary talents as a healer and teacher, the considerable force of her personality, and her astute business sense. It is impossible to count the number of students she taught, or to assess the impact of her teachings on countless lives, or to measure the power of the tide that carries the gift of Reiki forward. Those of us who practice, teach, and live Reiki cannot but pay homage to this remarkable woman.

—*Marianne can be contacted by phone at (206) 523-4456 or by Email at mariannestreich@mac.com or through her Web site at www.ReikiForLiving.com*

---

[27] Wanja Twan's ten-year-old daughter, Anneli was initiated by Takata to Level I at the same time that Wanja received Level II. Anneli took her own children to Hawaii to be initiated at an early age, although Takata was no longer living. Takata believed, according to a statement by Anneli Twan in a talk given at a Vancouver Area Reiki Masters Gathering, that the best age to initiate children is between four and five. (See footnote #15.) Sarah Baylow reports in an email to Rand dated October 22, 2006 that her mother, Master Ursula Baylow, initiated Sarah's son and nephew before they were nine years old.

[28] Wanja Twan, Web posting, www.morningstarproductions.ca/page2.htm
[29] Fran Brown, Web posting, www.reikifranbrown.com/bio.htm.
[30] Bethal Phaigh, *Journey Into Consciousness* (unpublished manuscript), 130.
[31] Robert Frueston, a student of Fran Brown's, in a Web posting, www.robertfueston.com *and* Johnson in an April 19, 1994 letter to Rand.
[32] John Gray, telephone conversation with the author, January 30, 2007.
[33] John Gray asserts that Takata taught only one attunement for Level II and that he added the second attunement method. See footnote #21 for Amy Rowland's perspective.

C E R T I F I C A T E

THIS IS TO CERTIFY that Mrs. Hawayo Takata, an American citizen born in the Territory of Hawaii, after a course of study and training in the Usui system of Reiki healing undertaken under my personal supervision during a visit to Japan in 1935 and subsequently, has passed all the tests and proved worthy and capable of administering the treatment and of conferring the power of Reiki on others.

THEREFORE I, Dr. Chujiro Hayashi, by virtue of my authority as a Master of the Usui Reiki system of drugless healing, do hereby confer upon Mrs. Hawayo Takata the full power and authority to practice the Reiki system and to impart to others the secret knowledge and the gift of healing under this system.

MRS. HAWAYO TAKATA is hereby certified by me as a practitioner and Master of Dr. Usui's Reiki system of healing, at this time the only person in the United States authorized to confer similar powers on others and one of the thirteen fully qualified as a Master of the profession.

Signed by me this 21st day of February, 1938, in the city and county of Honolulu, territory of Hawaii.

(SIGNED) *Chujiro Hayashi*

Witness to his signature:

TERRITORY OF HAWAII.
City and County of Honolulu. } ss.

On this 21st day of February A. D. 1938 before me personally appeared
* * * * * * * * * * *(DR.) CHUJIRO HAYASHI* * * * * * * * * * * * * * *
to me known to be the person described in and who executed the foregoing instrument and acknowledged that WHO executed the same as HIS free act and deed.

Notary Public, First Judicial Circuit,
Territory of Hawaii.

Notes

Appendix E

Reiki Products

REIKI NEWS MAGAZINE
DON'T MISS A SINGLE ISSUE!

We know that Reiki can make an important difference in creating a healthy and peaceful world. By spreading the word about Reiki and by providing quality information that serves the Reiki community, we achieve our purpose by helping you use Reiki to create a world where everyone wins.

We honor all lineages and schools and will focus on allowing the magazine to continually evolve according to the needs of the Reiki community. With this in mind we will be featuring articles from well-known Reiki authors and teachers as well as Reiki practitioners with important information or a story to tell.

Whether you are an experienced Reiki practitioner or teacher or you are new to Reiki, the *Reiki News Magazine* offers something for you. So, subscribe now! A subscription saves money and is mailed weeks before the magazine arrives on the newsstand!

SUBSCRIPTION RATES

Within the USA: 1 yr. $17.00 • 2 yr. $32.00 • 3 yrs. $47.00
Canada: 1 yr. $20.00 • 2 yrs. $36.00 • 3 yrs. $54.00
International: 1 yr. $25.00 • 2 yrs. $47.00 • 3 yrs. $70.00

We also have a perpetual subscription in which we will bill your credit card automatically each year unless you notify us to cancel.

GREAT GIFT IDEA!
A SUBSCRIPTION TO REIKI NEWS MAGAZINE WOULD BE A PERFECT GIFT FOR ANY OCCASION

Order your subscription today by phone
or save an additional 10% by ordering from our website.

Credit card orders: call (800)332–8112 or (248)948–8112
between the hours of 9–4 EST M–Th, 9–Noon on Friday

ORDER ONLINE AT: www.reikiwebstore.com

169

The Reiki Touch
A Tool Kit for Reiki Practitioners

The kit includes: DVD - Workbook - 2 CDs - Reiki Cards: $39.95

THE PEOPLE AT SOUNDS TRUE contacted me about creating a Reiki multimedia instructional kit. I was very excited about the idea and in fact, I had already been thinking of doing something like this on my own. So we combined our resources and created a really wonderful package.

The audio was produced at their studio in Boulder, Colorado. The video portion was produced on a sound stage using a specially constructed set. A crew of ten was employed including a producer, director, and camera, sound and lighting people. Working with such a tightly focused group of professionals was a wonderful experience and I am very happy with the results.

This is my best work to date and includes ideas and techniques I've learned from others, developed on my own and practiced and taught effectively over the course of 25 years. The basics of Reiki are clearly explained including the self-treatment, treating others, the symbols and sending Reiki at a distance. In addition, a number of the most advanced Reiki techniques have been included.

DVD

This one hour DVD includes the following:

TREATING OTHERS: Learn how to correctly give a complete treatment using all the standard hand positions. The glands, organs and chakras treated by each position are explained in detail.

SELF-TREATMENT: Follow along as I demonstrate the self-treatment — much like an exercise video. The glands, organs and chakras treated by each hand position are explained in detail and additional suggestions are included to increase the strength of your Reiki; help you relax more

deeply; and improve the effectiveness of the treatment. This is an excellent way to learn the hand positions while at the same time giving yourself a treatment.

BYÓSEN SCANNING: A Japanese Reiki Technique, Byósen Scanning uses the sensitivity in your hands to discover where the client is most in need of Reiki. A demonstration and clear, straightforward instruction is included making it easy for anyone to learn this technique. An advanced method is also explained that combines Byósen Scanning with Gyóshi ho enabling the student to scan with the eyes.

GYOSHI HO: Another Japanese Reiki Technique, which involves sending Reiki with the eyes. This technique enables you to send Reiki to anyone you can see such as a person on the other side of a room or outdoors and so forth. Gyoshi ho is an excellent technique for: treating children while they are playing, sending Reiki to various parts of your own body, or for use during a regular hands-on treatment to send additional Reiki where your hands are placed or to other areas.

SEEING AURAS AND PAST LIVES: This technique has been highly successful with over 95% of students getting results on the first try! Based upon Gyóshi ho, there are several reasons it works so well. First, because you are sending Reiki to the person's aura; Reiki strengthens their aura, making it easier to see. Second, because you are sending Reiki with the eyes, the perceptive ability of the eyes merges with the higher dimensional nature of the Reiki energy thus raising the vibration of the eyes and making it possible to see the aura and past life imagery. The demonstration and clear instruction on this DVD make it easy to understand and get results. This technique can be used with a partner or with yourself while looking in a mirror.

ATTUNEMENT NECESSARY: The Reiki Touch kit is meant for those who have taken a Reiki class(s) and received an attunement, or who are planning to do so. The attunement is a necessary part of Reiki training and is best experienced in person from a qualified Reiki Teacher.

170

HEALING SESSION: At the end of the DVD, I beam Reiki directly to the viewer using my eyes and hands. By simply sitting in front of the screen you will receive a Reiki treatment.

REIKI CARDS

A set of 30 uniquely designed cards that demonstrate the Reiki hand positions, symbols (but not the glyphs) and proper Reiki techniques. Each card includes a detailed description. The cards can be used like flash cards to help you learn the various aspects of Reiki. They can also be used to do a Reiki card reading. By following the instructions, you will be able to use the cards along with the intuitive power of Reiki to guide you to the best hand position(s), symbol(s) or technique(s) to treat a specific issue—for yourself or others. So often when we are in need of healing, the stress of the situation inhibits our ability to call on the full range of healing tools and techniques we have available to us. The Reiki Cards allow you to call on higher wisdom to guide your use of Reiki. I have used my own homemade version of these cards for years and it is uncanny how helpful and revealing they can be.

CD 1

This CD contains three Reiki meditations. As you listen to the meditations, you're asked to give yourself Reiki as you're guided into higher states of consciousness and offered new healing skills and energies. You will also be presented with the possibility of accepting an enlightened being as your personal guide. The first meditation increases the strength and effectiveness of your Reiki energy and deepens your healing process. The second creates a field of Reiki energy that surrounds you and protects you from all negative influence. The last meditation is for problem solving and creativity. The wonderfully soothing music of Nawang Khechog is played in the background of the meditations.

CD 2

This CD features background music to be played during Reiki treatments, featuring the flute music of Nawang Khechog.

WORKBOOK

A 100-page workbook is included that contains detailed information on every aspect of Reiki from basic instruction to the most advanced techniques. Sample chapters include: What is Reiki?; How it Heals; History of Reiki; Symbols; Treating Self and Others; Research; Byósen Scanning; Gyóshi ho; Seeing Auras and Past Lives; Increasing the Strength of your Reiki; Spiritual Protection; Reiki and Spirit Release; Creativity and Problem Solving; How to Receive Guidance from an Enlightened Being; Reiki and World Peace, and more.

 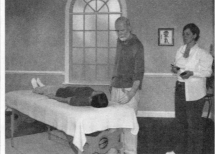 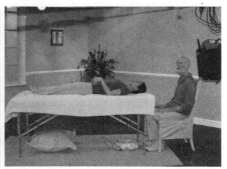

Cost for the entire kit is only $39.95
Teachers – 30% discount if you buy 5 or more.
Order now by calling 800-332-8112 or 248-948-8112
Or order online and get a 10% discount – www.reikiwebstore.com

Reiki
Master Manual

BY WILLIAM LEE RAND

In use since 1990, this manual has been continually upgraded to contain the most accurate and comprehensive information for Reiki Master training. Now combined with the *Advanced Reiki Training* manual, its 160 pages cover important aspects of advanced practice as well as providing a user friendly guide for giving all the attunements and teaching all the Reiki classes including the master level. Illustrated with more than 34 drawings and photographs.

- Origin of Western Reiki
- Reiki Moving Meditation
- Advanced Reiki Meditation
- The Reiki Grid
- Aura Clearing
- Origin and meaning of the Usui and Tibetan Reiki symbols including how to correctly draw them.
- Antahkarana healing symbols.
- Violet Breath
- Healing Attunement
- Detailed instruction on how to give all the Reiki attunements including the Usui and the Usui/Tibetan style.
- How to teach Reiki including class outlines and resources.

Used by over 2500 Reiki Masters as their class manual.

Spiral bound so it lies flat
ISBN 1-886785171, 160 pages, 8-1/2" x 11"
Price: $19.95

To order, please fax, email or mail a copy of your master teacher certificate. *Usui/Holy Fire ART/Master also available.*

Teacher Discount: Order 5 or more of same book and get a 30% discount

Order directly from:
VISION PUBLICATIONS, Southfield, MI
Toll Free 1-800-332-8112 or 1-248-948-8112
Order from our website and get an additional
10% discount, www.reikiwebstore.com

Reiki In Hospitals PowerPoint Presentation

We've developed a Reiki In Hospitals PowerPoint presentation to be shown to hospital administrators and staff that will help explain how a Reiki hospital program works. It explains Reiki, includes Reiki research, explains the benefits of Reiki and the various types of Reiki programs hospitals are currently using, and also includes a list of prominent hospitals that have Reiki programs and so forth.

Table of Contents

Overview of Reiki
- What is Reiki? Fable vs Fact
- Reiki In Action

The Science of Reiki
- Brief overview of the Touchstone Project
- Major findings and conclusions

Overview of Reiki's Potential as an Offering in Hospitals and Clinics
- Hospitals that have started Reiki Programs
- Potential Benefits
- Examples of Outcomes
- Types of Existing Programs

Resources for building a hospital-based Reiki program
- Contact Information

$25.00

Download directly from our website:
www.reikiwebstore.com

T HE ICRT REIKI MEMBERSHIP ASSOCIATION was created based on my then twenty plus years of experience as a full-time Reiki practitioner and teacher. Its purpose is to maintain a professional image for our members while at the same time preserving the spirit of Reiki and assisting members in creating a thriving Reiki practice. By becoming a member, you'll be associating with an organization that has the reputation of providing accurate, up-to-date information on the history, practice and scientific study of Reiki. Our published, user-friendly membership list is an effective way to promote your sessions and classes. And our code of ethics and standards of practice allow those seeking a Reiki practitioner or teacher to know that choosing one of our members will result in a professional experience. An online database to keep track of your classes and students and class certificates that include both the name of your Reiki center (if you have one) and the membership association logo are available to Professional Members. We also have an amazing Reiki insurance policy available with a tremendous list of benefits and at a great price. To create community, we provide a social networking page for members to share experiences and ideas with each other and an online Reiki share group. It is my expectation that all our members will do well and to this end I'll be sharing my training and experience with you to ensure that every aspect of your Reiki practice is as professional and successful as possible.

Sincerely,

William Lee Rand

Membership is available to Reiki masters in the US or Canada. Reiki Masters of any lineage are qualified to join as Affiliate members. Professional membership requires that one have taken Reiki I&II and ART/Master from one of our Licensed Teachers.

Benefits of Joining the Reiki Membership Association

Advertise your Reiki practice
Being a member provides an effective way to promote your Reiki classes and sessions. One of the features of membership is a user-friendly searchable list of members that will allow those seeking Reiki sessions or classes to contact qualified Reiki practitioners and teachers. We promote this list on the reiki.org home page, which gets over 3000 visits a day, as well as in the *Reiki News Magazine*, our online newsletter, and other prominent places. This list is becoming the most popular list used by those seeking Reiki sessions or classes. Since launching the site in early January 2011, our Teacher/Practitioner page is already getting 400 visits a day by those looking for a Reiki practitioner or teacher. This service is included at no additional cost!

Keep Track of Your Classes and Students
A benefit for Professional Members is a secure online database that can be used to keep track of your classes and students. You'll be able to organize them by class, class type, last name, and zip code and also extract email address lists. This service is included at no additional cost!

Print Student Certificates

Another benefit for Professional Members is the ability to create Reiki class certificates online and download them to your printer. Certificates are printed instantly from our member website and include your Reiki Center name (if you have one), the student's name, your name as the teacher, and will indicate your status as an ICRT Association Professional Member. A fee is charged for each certificate printed.

Membership Certificate

As soon as you join, you'll be provided with an ICRT Reiki Membership Association certificate that you'll be able to display on the wall of your Reiki room or show to prospective clients or students. This feature is included at no additional cost!

Social Network Group Page

Members have exclusive access to our Group Page where you'll be able to post notices and share information with other members. This service is included at no additional cost!

Reiki Brochure

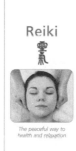

As a member you will be provided with a brochure to promote your Reiki business. This is a professionally produced brochure that clearly explains what Reiki is, how it works, what a session is like, and also provides scientific validation for its therapeutic value. The members' Reiki center (if you have one), your name, city, state, zip code, website, e-mail address, and phone are automatically printed on the back by our computer program. This info can be edited by members to contain the information they want. They are downloadable from our website so you can obtain them instantly and print them on your home printer. A version is also available for download that can be taken to a professional printer. The brochure is provided at no additional cost!

Reiki Insurance

A special Reiki insurance policy is available to our members. One policy covers Reiki and over 300 other modalities, including most forms of massage, bodywork and energy therapy. It includes professional liability, general liability (slip and fall), classroom rental, lost or stolen equipment, product liability and more! The policy follows you to wherever you practice or teach. Member price is only $149.00/yr.

Resources

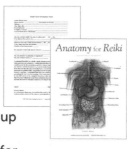

Our list of member resources includes: a Reiki exchange service that allows members to request distant Reiki for oneself, family, or friends; client documentation forms to help you keep track of your Reiki sessions; a full color "Anatomy for Reiki" chart; Reiki symbol handouts; and a list of articles to help you develop your Reiki practice, create a Reiki circle, learn how to work with animals or provide Reiki for the terminally ill. We also include an article on how to get contact hours for CEUs set up for your students. In addition, you will be linked directly to our Reiki Research Center, which will keep you up-to-date on the latest scientific studies and provide valuable information and tools to help you get Reiki started in a medical setting. All of these resources are provided at no additional cost!

To learn more about our Reiki Membership Association and to join, please go to:

www.reikimembership.com

ICRT Reiki Membership Association
Code of Ethics

1. **Confidentiality:** No information about the client will be disclosed to any third party without the written consent of the client or the parent or guardian if the client is under 18.

2. **Transparency:** Include on your website and be willing to explain to prospective clients or students your training background, what takes place in a Reiki session, the subjects covered in your classes, the amount of time spent in sessions and classes and the fee charged.

3. **Integrity:** Be honest in all your activities and communication.

4. **Support:** Have a friendly, positive regard toward your clients and students and openly encourage them to heal and to do the best job possible with their Reiki practice and/or teaching program.

5. **Respect:** Value your clients and students and treat them with respect. Never engage in any illegal or immoral activity with your clients or students. Never touch their genital area or breasts, never ask them to disrobe, and never make sexual comments, jokes or references. Abstain from the use of drugs or alcohol during all professional activities.

6. **Honor:** Honor all Reiki practitioners and teachers regardless of lineage or organizational affiliation. Refrain from making negative statements about other Reiki practitioners or teachers.

7. **Educate:** Inform your clients and student about the value of Reiki sessions and that they do not provide a cure and are not a substitute for care by a licensed health care provider.

8. **Refer:** Acknowledge that Reiki works in conjunction with other forms of medical or psychological care. If a client or student has a medical or psychological condition, suggest, in addition to giving them Reiki treatments, they see a licensed health care provider.

9. **Non-Interference:** Never diagnose medical or psychological conditions or prescribe medications. Never suggest that a client change or end dosages of substances prescribed by other licensed health care providers or suggest the client change prescribed treatment or interfere with the treatment of a licensed health care provider.

10. **Honesty:** Never use another person's copyrighted material in your classes, website or literature without permission and giving credit.

11. **Freedom:** Encourage your students to use their own inner guidance in determining who to take classes from including the possibility of studying with more than one teacher.

12. **Professional Conduct:** Always act in such a way so as to create and maintain a professional image for the practice of Reiki and for the ICRT Reiki Membership Association.

13. **Development:** Be involved in the continuing process of healing yourself on all levels so as to fully express the essence of Reiki in all you do. Be in agreement with and working to fully express the Usui Ideals and the ICRT Center Philosophy.

14. **Gratitude:** Be grateful for the gift of Reiki and for each client and student who chooses to come to you.

ICRT Reiki Membership Association
Standards of Practice

1. Use ICRT manuals when teaching your classes. Supply one manual per student. Manuals must be purchased from www.reikiwebstore.com.

2. Professional members: supply the RMA certificates for your students.

3. Reply to all Reiki related email and voicemail in a timely way.

4. Use a client information form and session documentation form in your Reiki sessions. (Available on membership site).

5. Create a safe, comfortable, harmonious space for your sessions and classes.

6. All training and class attunements must be given in person.

7. When teaching Reiki classes, use only the RMA Reiki symbols as drawn by Mrs. Takata for Reiki II and the Master symbols for ART/Master, which are located in the ART/Master manual. No symbols are taught in Reiki I.

8. Include time for lecture, discussion, demonstration, practice time and questions and answers in all your classes.

9. Reiki I & II can be taught together (Hayashi style) or separately according to teacher preference.

10. ART and Master can be taught together or separately according to teacher preference.

11. Require that a student have practiced at the Reiki II level for a minimum of six months before taking ART or ART/Master.

12. Use the RMA class outlines. Additional topics can be taught at teacher's discretion.

13. Minimum class times: Reiki I – 5 hours; Reiki II – 5 hours; ART – 5 hours; Master – 10 hours.

Reiki Symbol Quiz

Teachers Name: _____ Class Date: _____

Class Location- City: _____ State: _____

What caused you to take this Reiki Class: (please circle all that apply)

reiki.org Internet site   Teachers personal internet site   Open House/Reiki Share

From a Friend   Reiki News   Other _____

Please Circle Class: Reiki II   ART   Master   Karuna I   Karuna II   Karuna Master

Student Name (please print) _____

Mailing Address: _____ City: _____

State: _____ Zip: _____ Country: _____

Phone number: _____ E-mail: _____

Please draw the symbols for this class level below and/or on the back without looking at your notes. Be sure to include the names of the symbols. The numbers and arrows are not necessary.

Reiki I and II Class Review

Please answer the following questions as they pertain to the Reiki I and/or Reiki II class you took this weekend. Please circle your interpretation of the teacher's presentation of each subject listed below.

1- POOR –The teacher does not have a clear understanding of the subject being taught.
2- FAIR – The teacher's knowledge of the subject was very limited.
3- GOOD – The teacher presented the subject so I have a basic understanding.
4- VERY GOOD - The teacher presented the subject with more depth and detail.
5- EXCELLENT – The teacher includes a variety of information on the subject which may have included using personal illustrations and class discussion.

REIKI ONE CLASS	Excellent				Poor
Define Reiki, How Reiki heals	5	4	3	2	1
Uses of Reiki	5	4	3	2	1
History of Reiki	5	4	3	2	1
Gassho meditation	5	4	3	2	1
Byosen scanning	5	4	3	2	1
Explanation of self treatment, Byosen self scan	5	4	3	2	1
Practice giving Reiki to others	5	4	3	2	1
Kenyoku - Dry bathing	5	4	3	2	1

REIKI TWO CLASS					
Reiki symbol discussion	5	4	3	2	1
Explanation of symbols and their uses	5	4	3	2	1
Fxplanation of complete treatment with symbols	5	4	3	2	1
Client release, documentation	5	4	3	2	1
Koki-ho- Using Reiki symbols with breath	5	4	3	2	1
Practice giving Reiki to others with symbols	5	4	3	2	1
Gyoshi-ho – Sending Reiki with your eyes	5	4	3	2	1
Enkaku Chiryo – Distant Reiki	5	4	3	2	1

Did this workshop fulfill your expectations based on the class description provided by the teacher and the International Center for Reiki Training?   If not, please let us know in what area.

Did the instructor answer questions effectively and compassionately?

Did the class provide sufficient hands on practice?

What was the most positive experience you had in this class?

What Improvements would you recommend in the class or in the teacher's presentation?

NAME _____ (optional)
May we use your comments in our advertising?   YES   NO

TEACHER NAME _____

Please add any additional comments you have on the back.
Fall 2005

179